*W*hen you Face Your Beauty, you recognize that you are greater than all of the things you've gone through. The past no longer defines you, it transforms you. It is a deep knowing in the center of your being that you are loved and lovable. This sentiment is necessary to this life, and of inestimable value and immeasurable worth.

Face Your *Beauty*

Love,

[signature]

MELISSA R. HIBBÉRT

13TH & JOAN PUBLISHING HOUSE

WWW.13THANDJOAN.COM

13th & Joan books may be purchased for educational, business or sales promotional use. For information, please email the Sales Department at sales@13thandjoan.com.

Printed in the U.S. A.
First Printing, August 2019
Library of Congress Cataloging-in-Publication Data has been applied for.
ISBN 978-1-7331313-4-6

Dedication

For my beautiful Milán.

You are the greatest part of Me.

Your unconditional Love fuels me.

It is your Face that gives me meaning.

It is your Heart that gives me courage.

It is your Spirit that inspires me every day.

It is your Presence that makes my life possible.

It is your Being that gives me purpose.

I will cover you with Love wherever life shall take you.

I will reflect back to you how true love will rise within you.

I will stand with you and for you, to help you walk this life
Worthy when you show up.

And as you live, grow, and embark on your journey,
always remember who you are.

If you stumble, I will be there to remind you to give yourself
a second chance.

I will be right there whenever you may face failure,
to let you know there's always a chance to win again.

Most of all, my beautiful angel, the greatest gift I can give you
is to live a life that is authentic and filled with choices
that move me to be better,

and to accept the lessons, for they have transformed me
to be greater.

I will never apologize for standing in my truth—where my
true power exists from the inside out.

And that is when you Face Your Beauty!

Epigraph

That which does not kill us
allows us to tell a beautiful story of triumph.

-Melissa Hibbért-

PREFACE

Clarity

EVERY FACE HAS A STORY BURIED SOMEWHERE DEEP
WITHIN THE BOWELS OF THE SOUL.

-MELISA R. HIBBÉRT-

If you've managed to open this book, there is one thing that is for certain: You are alive. To be alive is to dance with possibility and potential. These two factors are unquestionably crucial to who and what we become in our lifetime. Throughout my life, I've been blessed to have a front row seat to the stages that showcased insurmountable greatness. I've also managed to discover the greatness that lives and thrives within me. But it wasn't until I committed to the process of writing this book that it all made sense. The real truth is that we all possess the same concentration of power and potential but, oftentimes, our pathways and evolution towards greatness are convoluted with the fog of the pain and trauma that we experience in our personal life. When relationships go from love to a dark place, and you find yourself in disbelief and questioning everything, your world shifts. This was the case for me. Having a clear understanding of our value and the vast array of gifts that we have to offer the world becomes the deciding factor as to whether or not we touch the hem of destiny and ultimately fulfill our purpose. Writing this book has illuminated the clear path of consciousness, healing, and triumph that I knew to be possible for myself and anyone in search of clarity. Clarity makes it all make sense.

I don't believe that we take our first real breath until we fully understand the patterns and experiences that have shaped and molded our existence. Clarity made its debut in my life in the form of what I now refer to as self-imposed transparency. Amidst naiveté, I understood transparency to be a game people played when they dared to risk it all. My rearing taught me that there was no safety net while walking the tightrope of lucidity, so I didn't. And I would be remiss if I didn't acknowledge that there was a bit of a haze from my adolescence that left me uncertain about various aspects of my life. This haze would eventually manifest in my thoughts about who I was, my value, and what I was destined to be and do in life. Coming face to face with moments of clarity proved to be the litmus test for my evolution. Today, truth has positioned itself as my point of reference for all things. And let me tell you, truth laced with intention is one of the most powerful combinations that we can implore as we engage in relationships and scenarios that are a part of our existence and ability to thrive. I've long heard it stated that the truth shall set you free—where there is freedom, there is peace. And if there is one thing that I am chasing today, without question, it is peace.

I was introduced to both truth and transparency by a woman whom I now revere as exemplary in many facets of life. I'll never forget the moment that I watched truth escape her lips.

She went on to detail the hardship that can ensue when those close to us bring us great harm. Her words pierced my soul and resonated with my heart and my own experience. In that moment, I learned two invaluable lessons. The first was that if someone who had managed to attain large-scale success still saw the value in sharing from the depths of her soul, there must be immense value in doing so. The second lesson that I learned was that transparency and the display of vulnerability was beautiful. The woman whom I speak of is none other than Oprah.

Like many, I've sat in awe while watching her earliest days of television. There she was, the purest reflection of myself, thriving amongst an audience that hung on her every word. Over the years, I took note as her levels of transparency seemed to intensify. She became an open book about being sexually abused during childhood, trauma in her teenage years, and being in relationships that didn't serve her—the more she shared, the more relatable she became. Her words, her courage, and her story gave me permission to share my own. More remarkably, it freed me from my own bondage of shame. I was in awe of her refusal to hide behind her pain. Quite possibly it may have taken her a little while to get to a place of open, unfiltered truth (like me). Nevertheless, she was there. Her truth made me a believer that I was not alone, and it's from that space that I now live my life. I am not defined by my pain; I thrive because of it.

It was a gift to avoid being alienated while searching for the strength to be transparent and walk in my own account of life. And this gift led me to recognize that I, too, was responsible for such an awakening in others who had been on a similar quest. I was called to beauty at an early age, and I've always known that beauty was power. There is something magical about the reveal—when she looks in the mirror for the first time and sees a more beautiful version of herself. She carries that confident energy over into the world. What is most revealing in those moments, where every brush stroke enhanced another feature, were the conversations and stories that were often not so glamorous. I knew in that moment that my purpose was bigger than my role in beauty—every face connected me to my client's humanity, and it was there where I felt compassion. Today, I recognize that we all have a purpose to help those with whom we come in contact with to release their chains. The common thread for each of us are the stories that we live, the moments that penetrate our souls, and the role that we play in our own perseverance. Every face has a story, and with the power and conviction of those stories, it is quite possible that there is also the presence of trauma or pain. Answering the call to go below the surface is what compelled me to pen this book that I now recognize to be a testament of faith. We must also recognize that we live in a content-driven society that promotes the reveal and unmasking of our truths now more than ever. This book is my contribution to the movement. More importantly, it is my deepest desire to change the narrative and remove the stigma associated with addressing every moment of life that can adversely affect our mental health and those that lead us to believe that we are somehow deserving of the affliction that we are often overtaken by. This book is a call to action for us to have the critical conversations about trauma and how it causes us to feel hidden and unworthy in a world where we have to show up and be seen.

I'd be lying if I said that my truths have always been front and center for the world. I was not raised to bare my soul at will for the world. I didn't have that open communication vibe in the household, so I kept a lot of things in, and certain experiences feel shameful to even speak about. My experiences, and many of the lessons that were passed down to me, demonstrated quite the opposite. I had learned that there was no safety net in handing your heart to people at leisure. I can attest to the fact that the mask, the wall, and the barrier that we grant ourselves access to, while in a desperate attempt to shield ourselves from the scars of life, becomes too great of a burden to bear. There comes a time when we can discover power in recognizing that the trauma we've survived and overcome is meant to transform us. Over the years, I have done the work to unlearn my earliest lessons about transparency and lay my burdens down. Aside from that transformative moment when I witnessed Oprah walk in truth, I can't say that there has been one moment in particular that made me arrive at the destination of truth. My life has consisted of a series of events that continued to reinforce freedom to fly after letting go of all that has ever tried to weigh me down.

It is this revelation that has brought me to such a time as this. Dare I say that writing this book and committing my truths to paper has been one of the most transparent moments of my entire life. There was no way that I could tell the story without acknowledging the truth that is embedded within. The good, the bad, and even the ugly becomes beautiful amidst truth because I am no longer bound by anything other than what is real. Truth is a gift that we far too often take for granted. I proclaim: NO LONGER! The time for acknowledgement of the pain and trauma in the name of triumph is now. We take our power, our joy, and our peace back. We face it all and move forward, living our best life whole, worthy, and loved—there is nothing more beautiful than that!

Acknowledgements

The title *Face Your Beauty* came to me in the middle of the night. I woke up, wrote it down, and went back to sleep. In the morning, I couldn't stop thinking about it. I didn't understand what I was supposed to do with it. Over the course of my life, my greatest ideas and inspiration have come at that hour. I now know it's the hour where God has my undivided attention. Over the course of the week as I kept praying for more to be revealed, it became very clear: This needs to be a book. I began to outline what that book would look and sound like, but I was stuck.

Fast forward four years later, and it is all clear to me now—there would be mountain given to me, to show the world it can be moved!

What I know for sure is that nothing in my life would be possible without the love and support from so many people: my earth angels who have helped me move mountains throughout my life.

To my beautiful daughter Milán: You are my greatest joy. You inspire me and make me proud. I melt when I hear you call me Momma. What a gift it is to share this life with you. The dream I had of you one year before you were even conceived was confirmation of how good God is to me. Now here you are, as beautiful, smart, confident, and bold as you wanna be. Baby girl, you are my reason. You are all my reasons.

To my parents: Mountains require strength to be moved, and there is no doubt that I was birthed by a woman with the greatest strength I know: my mother, Deloris Dallas. Inheriting her strength has made me the woman I am today—brave, courageous, daring, and bold. My mother has moved great mountains for all of her seven children so that our lives can be lived out to our fullest potential. She is the definition of how to sacrifice with love, and that selfless demonstration keeps me going on my toughest days. And to the only father I know, Rupert Dallas Sr., you heard my cry—literally at six-months-old in my mother's arms. I was not yours biologically, but that did not stop you. The true measure of a man are the choices he makes and the lives he impacts along the way. Your heart is bigger than your mouth, which is why you are a man a few words. I didn't understand that growing up, but now I get it. It's in the doing and the being that defines character, and that's the fabric of a man—a leader, a father.

To my brother Davin: You have been my friend, confidant, advisor, and partner in fun excursions. I thank you for being a great example of manhood as a dedicated son, husband, father, god-father to Milán, uncle, and businessman. Thank you for all that you do—some of my best memories of my lifetime were shared with you!

To my sister from another mother, Mrs. Karis Jeanene Stoudamire-Phillips: I could go on for days talking about how much you mean to me. You are the definition of sisterhood. I wish I had you in my life from birth, but you arrived when I was sixteen-years-old and, to be honest, that divine time was perfect. When you showed up, it was then that I needed you, and you have been present ever since. We have an unspoken bond that is rooted in unconditional love. Your friendship and sisterhood keeps me grounded. If ever I feel alone, I know Karis is there (with a glass of wine) listening, laughing, and sometimes crying with me. You have been there for me when I couldn't be there for myself—with love and resources, you make it happen. I didn't give it a second thought about who Milán's god-mother would be; you were my only choice. I can count on you, and there is nothing more beautiful than that!

This book would absolutely not be possible or completed in this life, without Mrs. Ardre Orie and 13th & Joan Publishing House. The minute I picked up the phone to share my story, she said, "Yes, let's do it." Our lives crossed paths many years ago, and now we are at a full circle moment—word by word of this book, she has blessed me, and I am forever grateful.

I truly believe that we are not alone, and that is why I could not have filled this book so richly without the brave and courageous souls that contributed their stories and experiences in the book to inspire and free others. I would graciously like to thank Sandye Lomax, Dunnie Onasanya, Katina Benenate, Keith Overton, and Camara Aunique. And most certainly, a gracious Thank You to my fellow Fiskite, Dr. Roselyn Aker-Black, for your professional and clinical contribution in the pages of this book.

A special thanks to some amazing people who stepped up selflessly with love, support, and resources during some of my toughest times (particularly in the past few years for my trials) emotionally, financially, and strategically: My parents, Rupert and Deloris Dallas, Rupert Dallas Jr., Davin Dallas, Larry Miller, Anthony Hawk, Sasha Gaye-Angus, Melissa McElroy, LaTisa Miller-Coleman, Yolanda Harris-Jackson, Karis Stoudamire-Phillips, I will never forget your grace and generosity.

I want to say a special Thank You to my social media family. Honestly, most of you I have never met, but you have shown me so much love and support over the years. Whether by supporting my products or businesses, showing up at my events, sending me the most kind messages, or writing heartfelt comments, I thank you. I also know many of you have prayed for me secretly. I know many of you cheer for me loudly in your own space. I am grateful, and I don't take it lightly.

CONTENTS

INTRODUCTION
The Mirror

COMFORT ZONES ARE BEAUTIFUL,
BUT LIFE NEVER GROWS THERE.

-MELISSA R. HIBBÉRT-

I'm sure you've heard the iconic name Tina Turner. Who hasn't? She has graced us with her imminent talent, and through her work, she has sewn herself into the tapestry of American entertainment history. In one of her many infamous songs, she references doing things nice and easy. I've always used her words as a reference for life and our approach to it. As much as we would all like to believe that every moment of life could be seen as nice and easy, experience has taught me that it can't. There are times when life will render you a rocky road to endeavor, and amidst those moments, the terrain is unquestionably fast and rough. All things considered, I have to tell you that those rough moments will force you to look in the mirror and take a closer look than you might have imagined. And as the saying goes... objects in the mirror are closer than what they appear. This is not a concept that resonated with me until I found myself at the epicenter of a relationship that no longer served me or fed my spirit...a relationship that vowed to consume me until I had nothing left if I had continued in perpetuity. That relationship forced me to set out on a journey that was fast and rough, but one that was also purposed to open my eyes, become brutally honest with myself, and fight like hell for my sanity.

What I do know is that this book is not composed for the purpose of serving as an easy read; it is meant to direct our attention towards the act of caring for and loving the person that we see in the mirror and to grant widespread awareness of a silent epidemic that kills spirits, taints souls, and smothers dreams: emotional and psychological abuse.

In all consciousness, I am well aware of the fact that this isn't the book that people would have expected me to write. The assumption is that my first literary effort would be an offering of makeup tips and beauty regimens. I would have to say that assumption is a fair one. As a makeup artist, and beauty entrepreneur, these are the factors that rest at the helm of what I do on a daily basis. Beauty is my life. What many don't consider is that although my business with beauty requires me to work on the surface of a person's face, I am also deeply connected to what lies beneath. This sentiment of connectedness rings true for myself as well as for my clients and those that I vow to serve. Behind the highlights, contours, and lush lashes, for some, there lies unhealed pain and the remnants of trauma. This has been the case for me. The pain and trauma that I speak of, unabridged and accounted for, is what lives and breathes within the pages of this book. After much soul searching, I recognized that there was a deeper tie that bound me to so many of my clients and to the women of the world who had suffered in silence. This connection is one that required acknowledgement and resolution for healing. This pain that I speak of prevents people from living their best lives and slowly eats away at the inner lining of purpose. This pain that I speak of diminishes our power, such that not even the fiercest makeup brush can conceal. This book is my opportunity to paint a different picture. Acknowledging the trauma that I experienced in detail has led me to resolve that the calling on my life is to ensure that we face our beauty from the inside out.

The idea of being vulnerable while sharing my story and sharing the story of others represents a triumphant moment in time. This book is living proof that I have resolved to come out of the space of shame and love in my light. It is my greatest desire that my transparency can be a beacon of hope for anyone in need of these words and the confidence to follow suit. If we dared to be completely honest, we would be inspired to admit that the reason we don't talk about the darkest places that we have encountered is because the sentiment of shame looms in the distance. Admittedly, I prided myself on demonstrating excellence, persistence, and consistency in my career and in my life. I resolved to seek the best methods of education to enhance my knowledge and hone my craft. I invested in myself. I am smart—dare I say brilliant—in my passion and dynamically walking in my purpose. And even though I am all of these things, I can say with the fullness of conviction that my choices in love were not so smart. None of the attributes that we revere so highly stopped me from making a choice that still affects me today. Not one of the factors that society categorizes as winning in life protected me or prepared me to recognize the signs of what would manifest as abuse. And even after you have managed to come to terms with your experiences, the shame continues through the unprecedented blaming of the very people who were victimized. You always hear people say, "Well didn't you see that coming? Didn't you see the signs?" When people ask me those cynical questions, it's almost like they're trying to infer that I am somehow dumb. I would venture to say that these questions do not come from compassion but more so from a place of judgment. Questions like this invoke the shame of which I speak. Prior to writing this book, I invested in the evolution of myself. I was forced to ask myself the hard questions. Why had I chosen a partner in life whose soul was not in alignment with my own? Why did I settle? What was I missing inside me that would attract abuse?

We can take comfort in recognizing failure as a part of our learning experience. Failure can happen in any aspect of our lives. And for the lessons that it renders, we can find power in being thankful for those moments. I've failed in business and with the execution of certain ideas that didn't work out. I've failed with girlfriends that I realized I no longer wanted to associate myself with. I've failed in sports when I didn't hit the game-winning shot. Waking up in the morning also means that it is possible that one day we might acquaint ourselves with failure. We are taught to get back up, dust ourselves off, and try again. I began to reason with myself and finally asked the question: Why should failure in love be regarded any differently that failure in any other aspect of our lives? Staring at the reflection in the mirror revealed that a better use of my time, energy, and internal resources was to understand why my marriage ended so quickly, and who I needed to be to move forward. Society places such a huge price tag on marriage and personal relationships that it feels more significant than any other failure, but the hard truth is that it is not. My life and the pages of this book are a testament to this fact. I can still hear the voices of my "spiritual mentors" while I was fighting my way towards triumph. Trauma didn't happen to me, it happened for me—I needed to get the lesson. Today, I have removed the mask and tossed it in the far distance behind me. A mask no longer serves me because purpose shows up on my face.

HEALING FROM THE INSIDE OUT

Some might ask what qualifies me to heal those affected by emotional abuse and trauma? It wasn't long ago that I found myself listening to Lisa Nichols one morning, speaking about life and how everything isn't related to the degree that we earn in a certified educational setting. There are times when we earn degrees by virtue of experience. The stories that I will share with you not only qualify me to heal those affected by pain but more importantly, they divinely call me to do so. In this perspective, I technically have a Ph.D. My Ph.D is what I now refer to as a

Personal Healing Degree. Although I earned an MBA formally in graduate school, my Ph.D from living this life and learning tough lessons serves to strengthen what I can offer to the world from an emotional standpoint. In both instances, I have done the work to earn both, and it is now time for that same work to manifest in the healing of others. One of the most profound revelations I had while working hard to study and understand my abuse is the science behind emotional and psychological abuse. This often helped me get a grip on why things happened the way they did and cast away my criticisms and shame about myself. In the past couple of years, there has been an emergence of topics and headlines exposing Narcissistic Personality Disorder and Narcissistic Abuse. As I was buried in my own suffering, I was also emerging in understanding—I was in a toxic relationship, and all of the signs confirmed it. As I began to heal through information, I was clear that these were the signs and patterns that kept showing up: One, they have no respect for your feelings and blame you for the problems. Two, they are entitled to all of you and all that you have, and they are explosive if it's not received. Three, you are constantly in circular arguments with them that make your head spin and manipulate you into believing something is wrong with you. Four, they will use your past against you to discredit your observations and confuse you with tactics to throw the communication off course. Five, you are constantly trying to prove your worth and forced to be the first to apologize every time. Six, they will shatter your boundaries, and when you try to stand up for yourself, you are criticized, rejected, abandoned and punished with the "silent treatment". Narcissistic abuse has a devastating impact on the brain and ultimately, the body keeps the score. All of these crushing experiences happen gradually over time, and when life happens, marriage, then children, you fight harder to stay for the sake of your family. But I wasn't willing to do that. I loved myself and our daughter's future enough to walk away and find peace. And what I know for sure is, the final stage of my healing is using what happened to me to help other people. That is healing in and of itself. I would be remiss if I did not answer the calling to share those lessons and the essence of transformation with the world.

THE MIRROR

Much of what happens in our lives is a reflection of how we process the series of events that we experience, the people that we encounter, the wants, needs and desires, and ultimately the decisions that we make that embody all of the aforementioned. When we stand in the mirror, we must ask ourselves if we are there to seek truth. The truth, ugly as it may be, is that there are many women and men like myself who have found themselves functioning in relationships that actively worked to destroy the essence of who we were created to be. If that sentiment rings true for you, I want you to know that YOU ARE NOT ALONE! Moreover, there is life after trauma. Like many of you, I was experiencing the love he thought he was giving, and I decided that's not how I want to be loved, so I'm out!

I wish so desperately that someone had taught me to recognize the signs of emotional abuse prior to committing to a relationship that would manifest in pain. If I can save one person by calling attention to every warning sign that I have ever experienced, then I can rest assured that this walk has not been in vain.

CELEBRATE

Freedom is the most powerful tool that we can add to our arsenal as we seek to overcome pain. Unbeknownst to us, we often blame the perpetrator in our lives for our imprisonment when in fact we are holding ourselves captive in many ways. While we must not diminish the actions of those who harm us, we must resolve to take accountability for the power that rightfully belongs to us. At the end of the day, we are all survivors and we've always had the power, but may not know how to use it. The key is to know that we have the power to survive. I want survivors to know that there is a way through the darkness, even if you experience a moment in time that you feel like you have lost yourself, your self worth, your self-esteem. There is always a way to get yourself back. The act of taking back our power in times that it has been compromised is synonymous with celebration. My ultimate goal is to celebrate every survivor and every heart who reads this book. I am committed to making sure that no pain is ever suffered in silence and that no purpose goes untouched. As long as we have warm blood running through our veins, our purpose awaits.

THE FUTURE BELONGS TO THOSE
WHO BELIEVE THAT THE BEAUTY OF
THE SOUL NEVER FADES.

-MELISSA R. HIBBÉRT-

B is for Breadth

THE ESSENCE OF LIFE IS TO BELIEVE
WITH CONVICTION THAT THERE IS A BRIGHTER DAY
BEYOND THE HORIZON.

-MELISSA R. HIBBÉRT-

I was born a lovechild, which means that even conception in infidelity couldn't shake the power of love infused through my DNA. My mom had a relationship with my biological father but later learned that he was married with an existing family, which resulted in his absence.

My father was even absent for my birth, and my mother was left to bear the brunt of labor alone. With the rapid onset of contractions and dilation, my mother delivered me with her own hands on the kitchen floor. She was a nurse, so it is likely that her professional training and instincts kicked in among other things. Even so, I would imagine that giving birth to and delivering your own child on the floor of your kitchen in isolation was no easy feat. My father saw me for the first and only time when I was about six months of age. Looking back on times such as these, I tend to believe that something inside of me was wise enough to sense the abandonment, even if I was unable to rightfully express the sentiment. That feeling would be forever ingrained in my spirit, until I later learned what to do with it. As for my mother, she eventually discovered a love of her own. As the story goes, one day my mother was standing in the middle of a store and I was crying profusely. A gentleman saw my mother struggling and stepped in to help her. That gentleman became my stepfather and the only father figure that I would ever know.

BROUGHTUPSY

An impoverished terrain in Kingston, Jamaica humbly served as the backdrop for my early rearing. By the time I reached the age of three, my mother left the country with hopes of laying a foundation to create a better life for my siblings and me in America. My new home in her absence was with my stepfather's aunt who would take on the responsibility of raising me. My stepfather's aunt and her family were domestic people who made their living by cleaning and caring for others. The work was honest but paid modestly. With so many mouths to feed, we were impoverished—often unable to make ends meet. The miniature hut with the zinc roof that they had managed to acquire was where we called home. My memories are laced with visions of our tiny farm equipped with roaming chickens that circled the back of the house. The inside of those four walls was equally humbling. I didn't have a bed in the traditional sense of the word. Instead, I can remember placing two iron chairs together and sleeping atop them at night and using an oversized shirt as my blanket. The law of the land dictated that we learn to use whatever we had to create whatever we needed.

Traditionally, the elders would see to it that the domestic skills that we so often witnessed would be passed down to us. In order for us to have clean clothes, we would have to assume responsibility to clean them ourselves—with our bare hands in a pan of hot water. I can remember a time when my stepfather's aunt was washing our clothes in an old tattered basin. I was sitting on a stoop and she motioned for me to come over. I immediately went to her and stood near. She looked up deeply into my eyes and said..."Melly, you should learn how to do this. You're going to need to know how to do this one day. You might as well start now, sweetie." Her words had weight in my spirit. After she stopped speaking, she got up to begin hanging the clothes that she had gently washed on the clothesline nearby. This routine had become second nature to her, and even at an early age, I recognized that it was passed down to us. Even so, there was something inside of me that didn't connect to the future that I saw in her eyes and heard in her voice. In retrospect, I'd say that I never believed that this legacy would too belong to me. And even though I knew that domestic work was what sustained me as a child, I couldn't help but to feel that life had something else in store for me, although I had no way of knowing what would be. Out of obedience, I assumed the position and began to wash the next soiled item in the basin, mimicking her every move. But, the warmth of the water didn't feel like home in my heart. It was a passion for her—it was her livelihood. For me, it was a way to show respect to my elders and towards those who vowed to invest in my rearing—nothing more, nothing less. Over the years, I would go on to add many things to my skill set that would empower me as I matriculated through life. I still scrub my floors by hand today. In addition to the physical grooming, I was taught by virtue of actions about the importance of self-preservation.

Whatever we grew or raised, we ate—we had fruit, vegetables, and chickens on our land. My favorite thing was picking up a warm egg out of the chicken coup. The little river in the back of the house proved to be useful, and next to it was an outhouse that we used as a restroom. There was no real bathroom in the house and no running water. Imagine as a young child, doing your business in the stream. That proved to be quite challenging. Boy, if that river could talk. It became my friend in many ways. I took my baths in the river and observed the constant flow of water. The most profound sentiment that the river emblazoned in my soul was peace. I knew that peace was a destination that could be experienced because of that river. I'm certain that as a young child, I didn't think of it as peace (as I lacked the language and experience to articulate it as such) but in retrospect, that's exactly what it was. And for one reason or another, it seemed that no one liked being in that river except me.

It is possible that I have always searched for peace in the nooks and crannies of the world. I failed to concern myself with the fact that I went to school in the same clothes every day. Instead, I found great pleasure in sitting at the feet of my elders. There was this little shop at the bottom of the hill that sold cooked foods like dumplings, fried plantains, and jerk chicken. They also sold, eggs, milk, bread, and other small grocery items. The walk home was filled with anticipation as I knew that they would be waiting for me and that they would feed me with no expectation of payment in return. Although they weren't my family, they cared for me and always made me feel like I belonged. For a young girl who was all too familiar with abandonment, they proved to me that family isn't always in the bloodline and love is unconditional. Maybe they saw something in me that I couldn't see myself at the time. All I know is that I was intrigued by those older than me. The fact that these people had tasted life longer than me made them more interesting than those my own age.

I also learned to recognize the signs of when my peace was disrupted. Around the age of five or six, I began to notice that the little girl who was our next door neighbor wore the most beautiful dresses and barrets. Draped in lace and vibrant colors, she was hard to ignore. I would watch her in awe as she danced in the distance and twirled to the sounds of nature in her front yard. On one occasion, I can remember gazing down at my clothes and recognizing the tears that had become an intricate part of the garb. I couldn't help but wonder how the little girl had managed to get so many beautiful items and I was left to create multiple outfits from a few tattered items. Although I wasn't jealous, I was curious and I can say that I would live vicariously through her—I secretly wanted to feel that joy, and I honestly wanted to put on something new, clean, and pretty.

Just on the cusp of turning seven, my mother returned to retrieve us after spending four years to work and save money. When my mother saw the condition I was in, she was heartbroken. It turns out that she had been the person sending packages filled with beautiful dresses and barrettes from America to Jamaica for me to wear. For one reason or another, everything ended up at the neighbors house and was given to the neighbor's child. I was old enough to experience the pain that she felt as the tears from her eyes rolled down her face. She was overtaken by guilt for having left me there in Jamaica to be cared for. I guess I could have assumed that she was neglecting me, but I honestly didn't know any better. I didn't know that she was sending packages to me; therefore I didn't hold anything against her. Knowing that she wanted to see me cared for better and that she attempted to do what she could even though she was five thousand miles away was what resonated most with my heart.

I learned in that moment that peace was an inside job. We often live on autopilot, taking in what is familiar and comfortable. Being on autopilot keeps us going at a comfortable speed, but what I have learned is that what matters most is to not get lost in what is transporting me because it will keep me from my truth and reality. Everyone near us lived in the same poverty, and some were content with their lives, while others were willing to compromise their morals and values to taste a different flavor from life. The neighbor being one of those on a quest for something different was willing to do so by any means necessary. She was stealing the packages sent to me by my mother and giving them to her own daughter to wear. I now simply believe that it was all a part of God's plan to teach me about peace and the power of not comparing our circumstances to that of another. It also taught me a valuable lesson at an early age to value what I have. Even if it's not as much as others, what I have has worth. And although I was grateful for all that I had learned and the love and care that was given to me, the house with the zinc roof was not my final destination.

My mother had returned in the middle of the night. I was not even aware of the fact that she was coming back. Today, as I understand it, returning to a small country after working in America can lead others to believe that you have had access to a great deal of money. Trying times often call for desperate measures. My mother knew that her return also meant that there were people who might harm me or abduct me to be used as ransom. It was startling to hear the stir of conversation and to be amidst the underground effort to get us all to America. Getting on the plane gave me that same sense of peace that I had always been in search of. The look on my mother's face was priceless. I think the peace had also found its way to her.

LOVE NOTE: LETTER B

The textbook definition of the word breadth is the distance or measurement from side to side of something. For me, the term best defines the capacity in my heart to love. Not one occurrence in my life has deterred me from the desire to vibrate on the highest frequency, which is the wavelength of love. I produce love, absorb love, and emit rays of love. And no matter what transpires in this lifetime, I vow to be the love that I so seek. My truth is that I am and will forever be the embodiment of love.

$\mathcal{E}$ is for $\mathcal{E}$mancipation

SHE WHO FINDS NO SHAME IN TRANSFORMATION
IS AMONG THE WISE.

-MELISSA R. HIBBÉRT-

SIXTEEN CANDLES

After moving to America, I came to the realization that the first man who was purposed to love me had likely marked me out of sight, out of mind. It had now been years being disconnected from my biological father, often left to question whether I mattered to him. This pattern of thinking became the backdrop for my sentiments about love. And by the time I'd reached the age of ten, I would venture to say that I believed that love was hard to achieve, or perhaps did not belong to me in the traditional sense. I'd often think of the elders in the store at the bottom of the hill, wishing they could have come to America with me—I knew love with them. I was now convicted by the notion that love and affection would not be given freely to me as I grew older; it was something that required me to work for it. This became an unwritten code that I resolved to live by. Because the void of a man's presence was filled, I didn't long for a father in the way that those who are estranged from a parent likely do. My stepfather was the only father that I had ever known. And although he was present, I'd be lying if I said that my relationship with him was without challenges. He was ten years younger than my mom, and he had taken on the responsibility of caring for and loving five children that were biologically not his own. In hindsight, I know that he did the best that he could with the circumstances. Deep down inside, I'm certain that I longed for a deeper connection. I would imagine that it was hard for him to nurture with the looming weight of what he was faced with. I struggled to connect with him and this left my emotional needs inept—he was present in our home but absent in heart and mind. I don't know that he had the capacity to produce outside of working and bringing home a check. The intangibles of nurturing, affection, and adoration was noticeably absent. Even the way in which he disciplined us didn't feel like love; my parents believe in the old bible verse, "Spare the rod, spoil the child." We were disciplined for everything, never feeling the innocence of making a childlike mistake. We were punished for simply exploring childhood at the expense of physically exhausted and emotionally impatient parents who worked up to fourteen-hour days, with little to give once they reached home. I learned early that love was akin to punishment; in order to receive love, I must also be willing to accept punishment. Somehow, they made the two intrinsically linked in the home and I hated it. The traditional daddy-daughter relationship that I heard people talk about was not my reality. And even though not seen through rose-colored glasses, we could never lose sight of the fact that he did indeed love us. His way of showing that he cared was to provide with a roof over our head, clothes on our backs, and food on the table. As an adult, I know now that he couldn't give what he never received. It's a tall order to expect nurturing, love, and affection from a grown man who still longs for that experience from his own parents.

I saw love in the old couple that would feed me back in Jamaica, so I knew that the expression of it was real. It just was not happening in my home. I'd like to believe that they were responsible for cultivating my ability to give and replenish love. Don't get me wrong, I was clear that my parents loved us - they gave us all they had and more, but as a child, my love language was different and my desires for nurturing and affection were unmet. Eventually, the number of bodies in our home grew, and the total number of children increased to seven. As the days passed, my mom evolved to be the main breadwinner, while in pursuit of a budding nursing career. With the daunting task of meeting the needs of seven human beings and maintaining a career, her availability for emotional connections diminished. As a young teen I found myself up late nights, typing her notes from nursing school, setting my own needs aside as a young girl to focus her desires—I inherited the role of my mom's school assistant, a job I really did not want, but how could I say no? Life was heavy laden. Ever the visualizer, I dreamed of greener pastures. I lived in my imagination most often and found myself vicariously experiencing moments through friends who I presumed had better lives than I. In my head, I'd made room for whatever possibilities I could conjure up and those that I'd witness play out in the lives of others.

Although there were many uncertainties, my ambition was not one of them. The desire to be and do more served as the driving force for my internal compass. Always in search of a way to make history, I had been the first of my siblings to do a church recital or engage with an audience through public speaking. The stage was a comfortable place for me. They would call me up to the pulpit to serve as the entertainment for the congregation. I have a photographic memory that would allow me to recite any scripture after seeing it only once. My favorite scripture to recite was Ephesians 6:11: "Put on the whole armour of God that ye may be able to withstand against the wiles of the devil. For we do not wrestle against flesh and blood, but against principalities, against powers, against the rulers of the darkness of this age, against spiritual wickedness in heavenly places." I was eleven-years-old when I first recited that passage, and I really didn't know the power of it, but I felt convinced that it was meant for me to speak over and over again and to believe it. I eventually understood that it was a preparation for what was to come.

Culturally, it's customary to arrive in America and reach back to Jamaica and help someone else come over for a better life. My parents extended an invitation to a friend of my step-father, a man he grew up with and wanted to help. This man arrived in America and moved into our home—he did odd jobs around the house to contribute while they worked on his papers. He was very fun to be around and showed a great deal of interest in assimilating into our family. At times, both my parents worked nights and he was left to watch us until they came home. One night, I was asleep when I heard my bedroom door open. I slightly lifted my head, opened my eyes to see him standing in the doorway—nothing was unusual about that because he often check on us. This night in particular, instead of closing the door and walking away, he entered my bedroom, kneeled down on the ground, and put his hands up my nightgown, into my panties and penetrated me with his fingers. He removed his hands from under my nightgown, pulled the gown back down onto my knees, looked me in the eyes, tapped-tapped my leg twice followed by a head nod. It was a subliminal message for me to agree to silence—to be sworn to secrecy trapped in his eyes. I didn't sleep for the rest of the night, or many nights to come. I lost motivation, I started to act out in school—picking fights with my classmates instead of the predator that I really wanted to fight. My anger was displaced, and I was ashamed at what my life had become. He made me experience a sensation in my body before I ready to. I was happy being an innocent little girl. I felt rage because I still had to see this man in my home every day as he pretended like nothing happened. The pain and shame silenced me, and I don't think anyone in my home noticed—not even my parents. They were too busy working to notice the trauma happening in their home, under their nose, by a man they spent their hardworking money to help. My siblings didn't recognize my new found silence either. Instead some of them made fun of me. While driving in the backseat of the family car, I'd gaze out the window and day-dream about the life I wanted, sometimes talking under my breath. They may have thought that I was crazy but I was praying beneath my breathe because I knew, even as a little girl, that my life and what I would become would only be what God called me to be. I stopped reciting in church; I no longer had the voice or spirit to stand up in front of the church. Shame became my companion and for two years, I did not speak a word in front of anyone.

Academically, I was an above-average student. I could have been better, but I was so consumed with my efforts to multi-task activities that, at times, my focus was diverted. On top of all of that, I was still living in the shame of that disgusting night. I didn't have the vocabulary to describe what it was, but now I know the words—I was sexually violated!

On a mission to chart my own path towards the promised land of self motivation and love, I can recall the moment I experienced infatuation. I was in middle school, and my neighbor was a chocolate dream with inviting eyes. It didn't hurt that he had a great personality and was fun to be around. Although I was intrigued, neither of us had an interest in a relationship, and we were likely too young to have a true definition of what it would mean anyway. Feeling the flutters that I experienced was proof that my heart was not damaged from being sexually violated, but I was scared at how my crush would see me if he knew my secret.

Our family eventually relocated from California to Portland, Oregon, and the last half of middle school and high school years would be spent attending Benson High School. We quickly found a new church home. It was a big church, larger than our previous. I felt God whispering to me that I need to break my silence on the stage by going back to my recitals. I went to church for weeks before I mustered up the courage to ask if I could recite Ephesians 6:11 the following week. The church organizer obliged. When it came time to speak, I walked up on stage, opened my mouth...

and nothing came out. I took a deep breath, and I could feel my tongue stuck to the roof of my mouth. I opened my mouth again, and began to recite the passage. I was fourteen, and this is still one of the most courageous moments of my life. What I know for sure now is, your abuser's job is to silence you, but like the passage says, "Put on the whole armour of God..." And that is what I did. I took my power back and found my way back on stage. I talked every chance I could get. One of my brothers used to say "Melissa, you talk too much," and I distinctly remember responding to him "I'll talk as much as I want to because my mouth is gonna make me rich!" He laughed in disbelief as always but after all, it wasn't his dream to realize, it was mine. Like most girls, my freshman year was filled with innocent crushes. I had crushes on random guys and the occasional bout of puppy dog eyes. However, most of my time was consumed with sports, and I fell madly, deeply in love with the act of using my mind to control my body and achieve a goal. As an athlete, I learned how to win, and winning felt like food for my soul amidst what some may consider a losing battle with the men in my life. My high school basketball coach was my hero—more than a coach, he was a dedicated husband and father. He made many sacrifices to drive the team members home after practice, delaying his time with his own family. He made us the champions we were, on and off the court.

After surpassing the rites of passage through the wonder years, high school revealed an evolutionary theme of independence. My mom and step-father's income combined were no match for seven siblings under one roof. As a middle child, it was not hard for me to get lost in the sauce. Instead of drowning, I resolved to create a lane of my own from which to swim. I can recall marching myself down to a local car dealership, just down the street from my school, and convincing them to give me a job. The gag was that I was not quite sixteen, but I gave them every ounce of maturity that I had acquired over the years. I answered phones and found dynamic ways to articulate myself in a professional setting. The typing skills I gleaned from helping my Mom with her nursing school paper proved invaluable—I boasted a typing speed of eighty words per minute. They put me behind a switchboard and honey, I killed it. At the age of fifteen, I was making sixteen dollars an hour. I was still a freshman in high school. My performance was so stellar that they would often try to let me go home with cars. Test driving new cars was one of the perks of working at a car dealership. Little did they know, I didn't have so much as a permit to drive. On one occasion, I indulged by driving a car home, and my parents were absolutely terrified. I'm sure I gloated a bit inside because I knew that my hands wrapped around the steering wheel of that car was symbolic for the maturity that I had displayed.

Recognizing my earning potential lit a fire under me. I even joined a temp agency and began doing administrative work for a major law firm who specialized in corporate affairs. The ambition kicked into overdrive as I continued playing sports and made the decision to go to beauty school. My schedule was hectic, but I surfed the waves like a champ. I would go to beauty school on the weekends, work at the car dealership during the week, and play basketball on my school's team on weekdays. The chaos outside of my home had become my new normal, but I don't think I ever quite adjusted to the chaos that ensued within the walls of our home. My parents were in a constant state of trying to figure out their relationship, while raising all of us. The stress was not subliminal; you could feel it, and because of it, home was synonymous with drama and unhealthy communication patterns. There were a lot of provisions, but a deficit of the outward expression of love. We had food in our bellies but nurturing is what I longed for. I did recognize that my parents weren't raised that way, so they didn't know what or how to give.

As time and fate would have it, my sea of calm was surprisingly disrupted by a random attempt from my biological father to reach me. At the age of sixteen, after acceptance of complete abandonment, I found myself standing in the middle of my room, reading a handwritten letter in which he was attempting to introduce himself. Baffled and filled with a surfeit of emotions, I held onto that letter for dear life. It was all that I would ever get from him.

MIRROR MIRROR ON THE WALL

Regardless of what was happening around me, I remained vigilant and very much a student of what was happening inside of me. Although I had championed every area of my life, I held on close to the prospect of finding that same sentiment of success with love.

And when I did allow myself to fall in love for the first time, it was like jumping out of a plane and building a parachute on the way down. The first guy that I classified as my boyfriend came into my life after I had assumed the responsibility of being an adult. And although, I was just about to graduate from high school, I did recognize that now, more than ever, I was responsible for the care of my own heart. In short, he was a really good guy that made bad decisions. While we dated my senior year in high school, our relationship was tested when I was a freshman in college and he had recently graduated from college. I resolve that he was doing what guys do. He partied and had different relationships with a variety of acquaintances. There was also some cheating that I didn't actually find out about until much later. It turns out he was rekindling a relationship with his ex on my watch. He was even bold enough to engage in these shenanigans while I was in his presence by disguising conversations with her as though he was conversing with any of his random *friends*. In my humble opinion, that constituted a different level of disrespect. I recognized that he didn't value me enough to refrain from having these conversations and, in retrospect, he treated me like I was invisible. I'd be lying if I said that it didn't bother me. Maybe there was something inside of me that wondered about his actions. Maybe there was something inside of me that knew he was dishonest. Either way, I had not made peace with the reality that someone could be so cold. The deceit in plain sight was ingenious. His actions were carried out right under my nose. To add insult to injury, he thrust blame in my direction. Instead of holding himself accountable, he became defensive about my justified insecurities and pain. He would question me, often asking, "Why are you being so nosy?" The unfiltered truth is that my new chapter with love left me feeling duped, discarded, and devalued. And then there are times when the party must come to an end. This was one of them.

A is for Acrimony

HEARTS STAINED IN ANGER CEASE TO BEAT.

-MELISSA R. HIBBÉRT-

SAY IT LOUD

I came. I saw. I conquered. There had not been a goal in my life that I had not attained. To say that I had a beaming resumé would have been an understatement. By the time I was ready for college, I was well rounded and experienced in handling business.

I made the decision with four friends to attend a historically black university in Nashville, Tennessee. I can still say that this was one of the best decisions I ever made. When I arrived on the campus of Fisk University, my heart was so full in knowing that I was learning amidst people who looked like me and knew our history. Historically, Fisk is the first institution of higher learning for freed slaves, established in 1866. Proudly, I stood on the shoulders of my ancestors, and when I walked the campus for the first time, I could hear the whispers of their joy in the soil and beyond the walls—I knew, I belonged there. I wasn't there long before I reclaimed my time with many of the same activities that had consumed my heart and my time in high school. I got involved in student government, planning fashion shows during homecoming week as well creating and hosting two shows on the campus radio station, WFSK. My shows were: *Jazz Hour with Miss Melissa* as well as another hour-long show called *The News*

You Can Use. Running these shows opened my eyes to another format for entertaining the masses. Maintaining employment while balancing multiple activities came second nature to me. Work for pay now took place in the computer lab, the credit union, and Saks Fifth Avenue Outlet. Although I needed the money, the other revealing truth for me was that being busy and productive meant that I was on the path to prosperity. All I knew was to be moving and working, and that's exactly what I did. I didn't embrace the luxury of the Spring Break college vacations. In fact, there was not one time during my college years that I indulged a vacation. I knew instinctively that it was important to plant seeds in the form of work while in college, and so I did. That old adage, "Actions speak louder than words," was my personal mantra. Taking control of my destiny had been the only way that I knew how to live my life and my secret weapon to sustainability. That same exertion of initiative that was woven into the tapestry of my life in my academia, employment, and the pursuit of my passion would also ultimately thread itself into my pursuit of love.

One day, a young man walked into my class, and I was completely smitten. He sat in the corner because he was late to class but that didn't prevent us from locking eyes with one another. After class, we connected through exhilarating conversation and felt mutually compelled to exchange numbers. I'd like to say that the rest was history. Shortly thereafter, we began dating exclusively. We were from two different worlds, but discovered synergy in who we were and the things that we enjoyed in life. Inseparable would have been the best world to describe us. We would visit his home, and we were constantly enjoying life and each other's presence. Whenever you saw me, you saw him. Even though we were college students, we were creating a life together. After about a year-and-a-half, and what seemed like infinite moments of growing fonder of each other, I learned about who he was on a deeper level, which also taught me about some of the internal struggles and the challenges that he faced. As the days passed, things started to change in his personal life. He had a very strained relationship with his mother that would often upset him to the point of frustration. Unfortunately, the negative energy tended to spill over into our relationship. He started becoming verbally and emotionally abusive. He would do things to get a reaction out of me, and I didn't like the way that he made me feel in those moments. At the time, I had not experienced this type of behavior, so I didn't know how or where to channel it. There were times when I considered that his background had exposed him to a great deal of trauma. He had witnessed domestic violence, drugs, and death in ways unimaginable at a very young age. It was certain that he was exposed to far more than I. Our difference in perspective also meant that I couldn't connect with much of was unraveling in his heart and in his mind. It was then that I should have ended the relationship, but being young and naive, I mistook trauma for compatibility. At the time, I believed I could build a healthy relationship on unstable foundations because that's what I knew in my home growing up. The truth is, I was fascinated by his wounds; they looked familiar. Instead, I should have ended it to seek someone who could stop my bleeding. I assumed that with this pseudo compatibility; since we hurt the same, we can love the same—boy was I wrong! In full disclosure, it really shook me up because he would get raging mad, and it was all displaced. He longed to talk to his mom but felt that he couldn't do so the way he wanted to. There were times when he would show deference and love and respect towards his mother and other moments that he would curse her out in anger. Watching him in this way was my first experience with trauma. I recognized how the way in which we are raised and our past experiences can directly affect our psychological state when we are suffering the most. It broke my heart to bear witness to a happy young man who was smart, bright eyed, energetic, and optimistic morph into a dreary, unmotivated, emotional wreck. My sense of compassion was heightened, but nothing that I did could change what had manifested inside of him. All of the lashing out affected our relationship, and things began to turn darker and darker until one day, the horizon for us was pitch black. The most daunting revelation that I discovered through all of this was that we have neither the power nor capacity to fix another human soul that is broken. There was a time when I got lost in the fairytale that I had discovered my soulmate, but then I was awakened by the reality that my sweet dream would end as a beautiful nightmare.

U is for Ubiquitous

THE MOST POWERFUL ACT IS CHOOSING
TO BE PRESENT IN THE MOMENTS
GIFTED TO YOU BY THE UNIVERSE.

-MELISSA R. HIBBÉRT-

Although college had taught me many lessons about love, my greatest evolution would reveal its manifestation through academia. I ventured from the classroom to the corporate office with ease. The same poise and grace that had allowed me to maintain a position at the car dealership and the acclaimed law firm while still in high school transferred to my early adulthood years. And with a successful career came a fulfilling relationship that reminded me that true love existed. The unconditional love and support I longed for came naturally from him—I was a Queen in his eyes, and he treated me like one every day. We traveled the world together and found a reason to celebrate the good in our life daily. Although our journey came to an end, because our long-term personal goals were not fully aligned, he still remains a true friend and confidant to this day. My career in corporate America served as grooming for my next venture. Eventually, I was moved to take the leap of faith with unequivocal confidence towards entrepreneurship in the beauty industry. Unlike the vast rolodex of the boardroom, I soon learned that the entertainment industry was interconnected and smaller than it appeared. In this capacity, it was true that your network was equivalent to your net worth.

After receiving a call from a friend who was a seasoned photographer, both the energy and intention to fulfill purpose amidst my second career was in motion. "Are you available to do a shoot for one day? They're not paying a whole lot, but you know it's a good look."

I was just starting out and eager to say, "YES!" to opportunities that proved to be a way to think, learn, grow, and make an impact. One of my mentors gave me a great piece of advice that sticks with me till this day: Whenever entering a competitive environment (in my case, the beauty industry) make an impact at an early-stage, and do it with persistence and passion—that's how you stand out! I accepted the day job with enthusiasm. After all, I was right where I want to be—called to do the work of beauty.

There I stood on the set of my first official paying gig, which was a one-day assignment as a professional makeup artist for the Oxygen network. The call time was something to the tune of seven in the morning, and it was located all the way out in the desert, which was how Californians referred to that location. When I arrived, I not only met the entire crew that I would be working with, but I also began to meet tons of other connections. I had never worked for a television network before in this capacity as a makeup artist, so there was a bit of a learning curve. As the day progressed, it dawned on me that I had been so engaged in observing and networking that I had not stopped for even a moment. I excused myself to the restroom and stopped to look in the mirror. I'm not sure if I knew to actually bask in the moment, but I can at least recall encouraging myself to own the fact that I was standing there. Had I truly reflected on how far I have come? Although never taken for granted, I was a far cry from the little girl who was placed two chairs together to make a bed in Jamaica. I wouldn't trade those moments for anything because they had managed to shape me into the woman who was standing in the mirror: humbled, thankful, and downright blessed. For the first time in my life, I was living life according to the terms that I set in motion. If that was what freedom felt like, I knew right then and there that I wanted more of it and that I was willing to work as hard as I needed to attain in my way.

After the pseudo-meeting with myself in the ladies room, I opened the door to return to my duties. I'm certain that I was smiling due to the powerful pep talk with myself. Just as I exited the restroom, my eyes were met with a piercing smile. There was no way for me not to have noticed him because of his proximity and subtle charisma that greeted me at the door.

I immediately straightened my posture, nodded my head, and walked swiftly back to my assigned dressing room. My first day on set as a professional proved to be even bigger. One of the producers informed me that I would have to be on camera during the scene as I made over the talent. I smiled and said, "Okay, no problem," but deep down, I was terrified! My heart was racing and my hands started sweating at the thought. Here I am, my first television gig, now on-camera talent all in the same day. Looking back, it was definitely preparation for what was to come in the future. We successfully finished a full day of production, and I could now officially log a win in the cache for my career as a celebrity makeup artist. It wasn't until after production wrapped for the day that I noticed the same gentleman whom I had engaged in the split-second standoff with near the restroom again. It was now apparent to me that he was a member of the camera crew. As all of the team members scurried to pack their equipment, he was noticeably searching for something that was misplaced, and I noticed him motioning for his fellow crew members to assist him in finding it. As fate would have it, I ended up stumbling upon the piece of equipment he had lost. I returned it to him, and I was glad to have helped.

My final moments on set would be spent enthralled in a heart-to-heart conversation with one of the talents who had been featured on the show. The nature of the show had been emotional, and I recognized that she just needed a moment to vent. Meanwhile, the gentleman who I had now encountered twice by chance seemed to be waiting patiently to talk to me. About ten minutes later, I would imagine that he had been observant and gathered that we had finished talking and that I was preparing to depart the set. With no hesitation, he approached me and said, "I wanted to be sure to give you my number before we all left." I gazed up at him curiously and uttered the words, "Okay. Great." He extended his arm to hand me the business card that he had been holding. I received it, smiled briefly, nodded my head while mouthing the words, "Thank you," and began to gather my keys and belongings to depart. And then, he broke the ice that exists between strangers..."Maybe we can meet up for coffee or tea, and I can pay you back for finding my camera equipment." Before I knew it, we were standing there laughing. Quite possibly, there had been a hint of tension in the air, but not due to anything bad. We were there to do a job, and it was apparent that we all took our crafts seriously. But in that moment, after realizing that our missions had been completed, laughter was welcomed. We bid our adieus, and I drove home, completing an amazing story that would serve as the preface of the next chapter in my life and in my business.

After sitting at home and reflecting over all that had transpired during the day, I decided to text the gentleman from the set who had given me his business card. It read something like..."Hey, I just wanted to make sure that you had my number too." He replied and the rest is history.

One might say that the innocent business card exchange and the text to reply in kind morphed into a friendship that he and I would nurture over the course of several months. I'll admit, there was a bit of chemistry there. Due to the fact that I was so new to the industry, I was largely skeptical about dating anyone who shared the same circles that I would now be a part of. That sense of hesitation also meant that he and I would not see each other for almost another two months after our chance encounter on set. Until one day, things changed.

We found synergy through our discussions about the industry, and his excitement about his new production ideas also excited me. After a repeated series of emails, we decided to meet for lunch. Even though everything about our exchanges had dictated a business meeting, I would venture to say that this was our first official date. Around one o'clock in the afternoon, we arrived individually and we hugged as we greeted each other. We decided to meet in Hollywood, and the scenery was befitting to discuss our hopes and dreams. When he sat down, I observed his eyes were a bit red, and I thought that I noticed the faint smell of alcohol. It was a little strange to me because it was so early in the afternoon. I remember inquiring—semi-jokingly, "You're not one of those partying camera men, are you?" He smirked and said, "No. I'm not that dude." I decided to take him at his word, even though my gut was sending me a different set of messages. I chalked it up to the fact that maybe he had been out late the night before, and I ignored the energy that my intuition had channeled. We spent the remainder of the afternoon at the restaurant discussing our hopes and dreams and plans for the future. Even though our conversation was fruitful, I could tell that I hadn't quite let my guard down. There were other moments during the course of the conversation that also gave me pause. He seemed to be overly fascinated with who I knew and what I had accomplished previously in my career. When things got personal, he was reluctant to say much, and my gut was saying *there's more to know*. But I also chalked that up to we're here to talk business, so the personal stuff could wait. I kept telling myself that I didn't want to date anyone in the industry but, quite frankly, he had piqued my interest. Had I listened to my intuition then, I would not be telling this story now.

SEASONS CHANGE

The more he and I talked business, the more our friendship grew. He was consistent, kind, and accessible. In all honesty, he was a welcomed breath of fresh air. For a person looking for love and romance, it can feel wonderful that someone wants to monopolize your time. He was also open, and we could talk for hours about most anything. Our discussions confirmed our mutual interest and, as time went on, I gradually put my guard down.

About a month-and-a-half later, we found ourselves on the heels of the holiday season. I'd imagine that everyone was feeling cheerful for a variety of reasons. My business was growing astronomically, and I was bracing myself for many booked months ahead. Our conversations led to an offer for a second date, and I obliged. This time, our meeting was prefaced as a movie and dinner with a good friend. The day after Christmas, we saw Django Unchained. After the movie, we had dinner where we kissed for the first time, and the laughs and smiles that we had discovered over the telephone were given new life over candles. We began considering more options to make time for each other. With the New Year right around the corner, more moments for us to connect were on the horizon.

I had no personal plans due to my hectic work schedule and was fully prepared to pop a mini bottle of champagne solo. I didn't even care about going to any parties because I had been so focused on building a clientele and sustainability for my still-somewhat-new future in the entertainment and beauty business.

I was a little taken aback when he extended an invitation for me to attend a New Year's Eve party with him. As he explained it, some of his friends were hosting, and he wanted me to accompany him. Based on my schedule, I knew that I would be working late which could mean that I would not be able to attend, or that I would be extremely late had I attempted. After I explained my disposition to him, his reply shocked me once again. "I will wait for you," he said. I looked forward to reconnecting in person and seeing how things with him might unfold. When New Year's Eve rolled around, he did just what he said that he would do; he waited for me. There is no way to not feel special amidst a gesture such as that one. When we arrived at the party, I didn't know anyone there and I was okay with that. He accommodated me and, through my observation, I realized that these were not just random friends. He had invited me to share time and space with his true circle. The party was filled with people that he seemingly had known for years and many whom he had grown up with. There we were, on the cusp of a new year, standing arm in arm, encircled by trust, saying goodbye to one year and welcoming in another.

Together, hand in hand, we found ourselves screaming, "Seven, six, five, four, three, two, one...Happy New Year!" Bringing in the New Year with him established a deeper bond. I also felt that the act of bringing me around his friends so soon meant that he felt that I was special. In my mind, this was only something that happened much later in relationships, but we were on the fast track to a destination that I could not have predicted.

In the New Year, things remained the same, and we put forth a more concerted effort to make time for each other. As February rolled around, he had to leave town for a few weeks to go shoot a show. Nothing changed about our communication, but everything changed about the way that we felt about each other. We video called each other every single night—never missed a day, and our nights ended seeing each other on the other end of the phone. No longer positioned as a friendship, we were posturing ourselves for a budding relationship with exclusive terms. There was one moment, however, that was perplexing. During a video call one evening, I couldn't reach him, somehow the calls were bouncing to another line. I called twice and the called picked up, but no one said anything. I waited a bit longer, called again. This time, someone picked up. The voice said, "If you're trying to reach my husband, this isn't his phone." I gasped and quickly hung up. Later that night, he called me, I told him what happened during my call earlier, and he gave me a lengthy explanation and assured me it was no big deal—it was not his wife, but his "ex-wife" who's email was still linked to his email which transmits the video call. Although I felt it to be odd, and my gut was telling me something was off, I romanticized that moment by giving him the benefit of the doubt. After all, in four months, he'd given me no reason not to trust his words. Our daily video calls continued; the more we talked, the more I felt connected. He used the time to share with more about his life and I, for the first time in a long time, felt opened up. I was somewhat taken aback by the fact that we were both still so interested to each other, even while not physically present and sharing the same space at times. The pace of our relationship picked up, and the romance transitioned from steady to whirlwind! Once he returned from his trip, we started sharing more energy, time, and space.

As spring rolled around, I can recall gazing out of the window of the passenger's side of his car. We we were on a roadtrip to Southern California to meet his family for the first time. That day, he officially asked me to be his lady, and he told me he loved me.

Our conversations were no longer surface and channeled now more towards where we were both positioned in our lives and what we wanted for the future. He shared intimately with me about his previous marriage that didn't work out. I had never been married before, so it was interesting to hear his perspective. There were many commonalities in our train of thought but also recognizable differences in our experiences. He had experienced the joys of fatherhood, and I was eager to receive the gift of motherhood. We discussed the prospect of children together as it had always been a desire of my heart. He was a little ambivalent about the topic because he was getting older, and I understood. His experiences didn't remove or even alter my desire to be serve as a vessel for new life. For a while, we agreed and resolved to build life hand in hand. The relationship continued to evolve, and I was pleased to introduce him to my family. We even began collaborating on projects together. I would even venture to say that the industry saw us as a couple to envy. In the entertainment business, you don't often see dynamic black couples in production. People loved and respected us for that. The more that we grew as one, the more intense my desire became to nurture a family under our union.

A shift in the relationship would be realized when the aftermath of his previous marital failure began to weigh on him. He started to get agitated around the conversation about more children. It appeared to me that his thinking started to change, and his apprehension about having more children grew. We were drowning in a haze of confusion. This also meant that the conversation about marriage came to a screeching halt. I had no intention of marrying a man without the prospect of having children. For me, marriage also meant that a baby was a part of the plan. One day, amidst a now routine contentious discussion, he said, "I honestly don't think I want anymore children." We both knew that all bets were off and, just like the weather, the season of our love had changed.

SOMEWHERE OVER THE RAINBOW

After moving out of the space that he and I shared, the anguish of loss showed signs of fading. The dreaded seconds of silence turned into hours and the hours turned days and I learned to count on myself once again as I had always done. Before I realized it, six months had passed. With love in my soul and hope in my heart, I discovered love again. Within a few months of dating, my courtship resulted in a proposal. I accepted and channeled all of my energy and intention towards creating the life that I so desired. And even the best kept secrets have a way of surfacing on social media. My ex caught wind of the engagement and, suddenly, the man who had once offered me silence now wanted nothing more than to talk. I had never seen him so devastated and distraught. From what I had witnessed growing up, it was rare to see a man cry. I had been under the impression that they were not as emotional as women. His expression of brokeness spoke to a place in my heart that even his words had not managed to touch. In hindsight, I now know that I felt like maybe our business was unfinished. A surge of hope was instilled in my soul that our desires for a family together were coming full circle. The cyclonic wave of emotions made me begin to question everything. There was a presence of intrepedition in my new relationship that I had not previously experienced.

I was torn and fighting an internal battle. The prospect of breaking someone's heart after having experienced it firsthand made my spirit restless. Ultimately, there is no blueprint for love. If I moved forward with the engagement, I might have always wondered about what could have been. At the back of my mind, I also knew that my ex and I had unfinished business.

There was also no way for me to not question whether or not I was making a bad choice by getting married so quickly. Would I have been compromising my fate or falling out of alignment with God's will for my life if I hadn't taken the time to at least hear him out? After careful consideration, I came to terms with the fact that this was a lane that I felt compelled to allow my heart to drive in as opposed to my head. Ending the engagement felt right in my soul because the unabridged truth is that my heart was still with my ex. And although I admittedly felt regret, there was no way that I could blame myself for not living in two worlds. I had to make a decision one way or another, and I did.

In a twist of emotion and ambitious love, I ended my engagement and resolved to love my ex even harder. I wanted nothing more than to heal us and to be fruitful in our union.

In each other's arms again, things seemed to fall right back into place. It was like we had never even skipped a beat. His family was happy we were back together. My family was happy we were back together and, without hesitation, the engagement happened. As for the engagement, it was a romantic as it was going to be— in a private park, on a blanket, shortly after eating shrimp tacos. I thought surely, we were having a picnic, but a moment later, he started to reach into his backpack. I could tell, his mood changed and his eyes were hazy. He reached for my hand, held it tightly, and began to proclaim his love but also his desire to be in a marriage where he could "be himself" and be "accepted for who he is." He talked about all the happy times and peace he wanted for his life. And then...the words every woman wants to hear. *Will you marry me?* He opened the box, revealing the ring—it's the exact one I wanted. I looked him in the eyes and said "Yes!!" We hugged and kissed and hung out in the park for a few more hours. It was one of the happiest moments of my life. Once he proposed to me, the normal progression of planning ensued, but ours was on steroids. I was ready to build a life and to start a family of my own.

T is for Traumatization

EACH OF US CARRY WOUNDS THAT NEVER SHOW ON
THE BODY. INSTEAD, THEIR PRESENCE CAN BE FELT
WITH THE SOUL.

-MELISSA R. HIBBÉRT-

Reconciling my relationship was the epitome of a crucial era in my life. As I approached my fortieth rotation around the sun, I was eager to begin the next chapter. My sentiment was such that we didn't need to put our lives together off for another second. Six months after getting back together, we were married. There was such euphoria about our lives that made its presence felt. Looking back, I now believe that it was the aura of second chances and new beginnings. I never expected perfection, as I knew that marriage meant fusing two imperfect people to create one bond and one union. Even so, there were some things that felt off for me. I ignored everything that had the potential to compromise the joy I felt. What I failed to realize was that I was often alone in that quest for joy. The excitement shielded the fact that I was alone in the process of planning the many aspects of the wedding. From date of wedding, to the selection of the location, to the type of flowers and reception venue, the decisions rested on my chest. I could have deduced that some men would opt to not be as involved deeply in the planning process, but I never expected what felt like complete absence of his energy. There was also some friction regarding how the expenses were allocated. He was much more frugal than I. He also felt a sense of stress due to the holidays being right around the corner. We were trying to piece it all together financially. He expressed openly that he did not desire to have what he referred to as a lavish wedding. For me, a wedding was a dream come true. He made the process more stressful than enjoyable by challenging everything I planned.

The day of the exchange of nuptials carried a different surge of energy. We were both present and basking in the residue of love. Bliss had managed to overtake every other sentiment that had been present prior to that day. I woke up looking at my beautiful Stephen Yearick hand-beaded wedding gown that my mom purchased—I personalized it by an extra crystal strap for more added elegance. I loved my dress! What's more, my swarovski crystal bouquet holder with my initials was gifted to me by a fellow entrepreneur who reached out to me online. Inside my bouquet were two dozen red roses, strategically placed to fill the bouquet—it was stunning. I completed my bridal look with a cathedral length veil, with a custom crystal crown—every detail was covered. Surrounded by a small gathering of friends and family, the day felt magical. Amidst the calm, the heavens opened up and allowed the presence of a storm. The rain imparted more stress, and I wasn't sure if everything would go as planned. Just as I had began to lose hope, the clouds parted and the sun broke through. It was like God showed up in that moment. We did first looks, and he was overwhelmed by how I looked. It was truly of those beautiful moments where I truly felt God was with us. The wedding was beautiful, our vows were unique and untraditional. We also hosted an intimate five-course reception dinner at a beautiful restaurant in Santa Barbara. And so it was, we vowed before beloved witnesses to love and honor each other eternally amidst both sunshine and rain.

Exchanging our vows right before Thanksgiving meant that we were bracing ourselves for another holiday season, this time as husband and wife. Together, we had one of the most incredible Christmas holiday seasons that I've ever experienced. Everything seemed so special amidst our marital bliss. Inspired by our hopes and dreams, we made a ton of resolutions and promises together. Taking special care to carve out areas of focus for behaviors that we either wanted to see more of or alleviate became an integral part of our union. We resolved to be healthier and stronger. He resolved to drink less, and I resolved to argue less and communicate more. Riding the wave of the honeymoon high also meant that behaviors could more easily be swept under the rug. I can't say that the drinking stopped as much as I wanted it to—I didn't like how the energy changed when alcohol was present. To be honest, I've always enjoyed a cocktail or good wine, but the presence of it in my system didn't change my behavior. But for him, it did. There were moments when he wouldn't drink at all and he promised me he'd "slow down" and others where he would revert back to his old ways, and so would I. These moments almost always ended in arguments, and I was always to blame for "bringing it up and not letting him be a man." I walked on eggshells often and bit my tongue because I didn't want to "be the problem." I wanted peace, and if what he called a "nightcap" every single night, two or three times a night made him happy, I had to fall back on my feeling about it. During this same time, we were trying to conceive. I thought this to be important to both of us, which was another reason that I fought tooth and nail for him to slow down with the drinking. In February, the month of love, our bond was forever bound through a divinely-appointed gift from God. I remember the fateful day I was driving home from my esthetician class and I just felt different. My body and appetite that day was not normal. I couldn't eat the tuna nicoise salad that I normally enjoyed, my head was cloudy, and I was just unsettled all day. My body was speaking to me and I listened. I got off the off the highway, went straight to the drugstore, and purchased two tests—an extra one for backup. As soon as I entered our home, I ran to the bathroom and took the test. It was the longest two minutes of my life. My heart was racing and my palms were sweating. I was pacing back and forth. And then, the pregnancy test confirmed that the miracle of life was within me. I started crying and screaming and thanking God for his blessings. I could not stop crying tears of joy, not only because I was happy beyond belief, but because had I listened to the naysayers who were trying to convince me that my forty-year-old body's eggs were "old," I would never have experienced this miracle. So much negative attention is directed toward women who conceive over the age of forty. Women at this stage in life are made to believe that natural conception is not an option or that the chances are very limited. All the negative stuff they put in your head had been deleted almost instantly from mine. I was elated, and I couldn't wait for him to come home and to share the beautiful news.

He was working on assignment out of town when I discovered that I was with child. Engulfed by excitement, I called him. He was happy but there was also the presence of shock in his voice. It was almost as if what I was saying was unbelievable. For the life of me, I couldn't figure the anxious disposition of his voice. Had he returned to his earlier train of thought in not wanting children? It broke my heart that he did not seem to share in the sense of extreme excitement that I was caught up in the rapture of, but I also knew that people react to different moments in life in different ways, and I was confident that his reaction was not a reflection of our plans or the baby. It was one of the happiest moments of my life, and there was nothing that could have come between the sense of fulfillment that I felt from knowing that there was a little heartbeat inside of me. On October 26, 2017, I gave birth to Milán Zahara whose presence illuminated my life. That day was and still is the happiest moment of my life.

My pregnancy was beautiful. I fully embraced that my body was now the home of little human for the next nine months. I changed my lifestyle immediately in terms of my diet, social activities, wellness, and self-care. I drank a gallon of water a day—something I have never done in my life. I never missed a day of my prenatal vitamins, I embraced prenatal yoga, and listened to a lot of spiritual music. Due to falling in the category of "high risk" because of my age, I had many more appointments that the average person. After passing the dressing twelve-week mark, I was in the clear. The best appointment was just around the corner: the day I heard the most beautiful sound of my life— her heartbeat for the first time. Talk about magic! And from that day for thirty-six weeks, at every appointment I loved to hear her beating heart each time. I loved being pregnant—my body was radiant. My skin was glowing, my hair was growing and, in the end, I did not develop any new stretch marks. The other fun element for me during my pregnant was the kindness of strangers to a pregnant woman! Random strangers opened up doors for me, carried my bags, gave up their seats, offered me beverages, and so many other expressions of care and concern. Looking back, it was almost as if God was sending me these angels so that I wouldn't ultimately feel alone in my pregnancy. There was always someone there for me, even if I did not know their names. The nesting was wonderful. I designed her nursery fitting of a little princess—I was so proud to walk by her room daily knowing that, one day soon, I'd be changing her diaper, feeding her, and rocking her to sleep in her room. The morning of October 26th, I woke up to use the bathroom. As I began to walk back to my room, a gush ran down my legs, and I knew right away that my water had broken. I woke up my then husband at said, "It's time." His reaction was funny because, just like me, he was confused and startled—it was surprising. My due date for Milán technically was thirty days away, but apparently she couldn't wait to get here. I called my doctor and my mother (she booked the first flight out) we both got dressed quickly, grabbed the hospital bag (thank God I packed it in advance) and we were on the road to Cedar Sinai Hospital. I was in the hospital for only a couple hours before I was fully dilated and it was time to push. Within seconds, the room was filled with my doctors, nurses, NICU doctors—at that point, I was in so much pain that I didn't mind the crowd. I just wanted to push. My doctor said, "Relax and let's have this baby." After seven minutes of pushing, the most beautiful angel entered the world. The doctor placed her on my bare chest, and my life was forever changed.

The elation of being a new mom is indescribable. My mom arrived at the hospital seconds after I gave birth, and we celebrated the moment together. Three generations hugged up on the hospital bed—it was beautiful. Two days after giving birth, it was time to take our baby home. I couldn't wait to introduce her to the nursery that I designed with love. I prayed in that empty room many mornings, creating a spiritual atmosphere in the walls that would be her own sacred place. Once we arrived home from the hospital, I took her into the nursery for the first time. My mom helped me with her—she was so tiny and fragile, and I just wanted to do everything right. Minutes later, in walks my then husband, into her sacred room, with a glass of wine—he placed it on the nightstand, sat down, and kicked his feet up. I was livid! Not even the presence of our new born baby, in her sacred space, could encourage him to make better choices and respect my wishes and our home. For some, it may seem trivial to take issue with a seemingly-celebratory glass of wine, but behind closed doors, I know how alcohol plagued our relationship and marriage. I know the monster he became and the agony I had to endure, and those experiences are not trivial to me at all. And like every time before, when I challenged his behavior, he would treat me badly, and the stress was the last thing I needed just days after pushing a human from my body. That same stress led my milk to dry up. I couldn't breastfeed after a couple weeks, and that was devastating! I wanted badly to experience the bonding of breastfeeding my new baby. I had one of the best lactation specialists at my disposal, but there was nothing she could do— she said there was a direct correlation between life stress and breastfeeding outcomes. Eventually, I was at peace with the reality that breastfeeding was not an option, but what mattered most is that she was fed and healthy. Being a new mom also meant sleepless nights, of which I totally understood. What I could not comprehend was being left alone while he moved into the guest room—his explanation was that he needed rest and wanted to give us space. Yes, you heard me correctly: He needed rest! I never got a break, and my body was taking on a lot in such a short period of time after giving birth. The toll of that resulted in being admitted back into the hospital to be treated for postpartum preeclampsia. The night before I went to the hospital, I couldn't sleep because my body was in excruciating pain. I knocked on his door a few times to tell him I was in pain. He brushed it off and said, "Stop being a drama queen." I couldn't even lay down on my bed because the pain in my back was so severe, my feet were swollen, and I had shortness of breath. The voice in my head said, *You need to go to the hospital.* That morning as he was getting dressed for work, I started crying on his shoulder because the pain in my body was unbearable. I told him I needed to go to the hospital. He said, "Okay. I'm going to head to work, so keep me posted." I looked at him with sadness. He couldn't even see that my pain was real. He couldn't get past his own agenda to care for me in that moment. I was sad, disappointed, and truthfully angry. So I put on some clothes, packed the diaper bag, and with excruciating pain, I drove myself and my three-week-old baby to the emergency room. Minutes after arriving, I checked into a room, they ran some tests, gave me the diagnosis of postpartum preeclampsia— a term I never heard of in my life. I needed to be informed right away, so I grabbed my phone and googled the term. Turns out, it's very common among African American women. Postpartum preeclampsia is a rare condition that occurs when you have high blood pressure and excess protein in your urine soon after childbirth. Another form of trauma entered my body and with concern in their eyes, the nurses told me that I need to be admitted immediately and would need to go on morphine and magnesium to bring down my blood pressure. Before I knew it, I was hooked up about four IVs, fighting for my life with an infant tucked beside me. The nurse told me if I had arrived any later, I would have endured a severe stroke, developed seizures, or death. Thank God I listened to my body!

AS THE WORLD TURNS

Seasons change. People change. Even with a beaming new baby, things between us went bad quickly. I no longer recognized the person that I fell in love with and married, and that hurt like hell. It left me wondering if he came back into my life for love or revenge? I remember one day I looked up at the calendar and realized that it had been fifty-three days of "silent treatment." I now know that this is an extreme form of emotional abuse. I could only assume that he was reacting to me in this way because I was holding him accountable for things he said he would change. Then there was the "gaslighting". He'd come home late and wake me and the baby up with loud noise. When I'd ask for help putting her back to sleep, he would say, "That's the job you signed up for, so deal with it." On other nights, he'd kick my bedroom door open when the baby and I were sleeping. After I jumped up out of fear, he would then record my reaction. My therapist told me he was doing that to try and frame me if I responded negatively. This is called "reactive abuse". There was also a series of stalking incidents. He'd strategically place recording devices to listen and watch my every move in our own home. Can you imagine a month-and-a-half in a home with an infant, where there is no communication and walking on eggshells, suffering in silence, while searching for an end to the torture? This was my life. If hell had an address, it would have been our home. It was a dark place—the lights continued to dim in our beautiful home. The only thing that I felt that I had working towards my advantage was the strength produced amidst knowing that I was now responsible for a life in addition to my own. Our beautiful daughter saved me! As an infant, she was sweet, gracious, calm, and loving, and she still is! Being her mother brings me so much joy—I couldn't wait to dress her up in little tutus and turbans, even if we weren't going out. It was always a photo shoot in the house. I leaned into motherhood, which kept me from losing myself. I vowed, even before she was born, to be a shining example of womanhood, even if that meant that Mommy had to make some tough choices for peace. I allowed every decision that I made from that point forward to be rooted in strength and the promise of a better tomorrow for me and her. I remember one morning sitting on the balcony, sippin on green tea. I looked down to see my neighbors taking their usual morning stroll hand-in-hand while pushing a stroller. With tears in my eyes, it dawned on me: "I am now a single mother." Truth is, I wanted to leave many times during my pregnancy—to reduce the stress on my body, to protect my daughter's spirit in the womb, and to be in a safe space. Statiscally, it takes a person seven times to leave before they do for good. It's more complex than people realize. Like many women, I was seemingly trapped financially because my work had to decrease as my stomach increased, so I tried to make the best of it while holding on to the little money I had of my own. For the sake of our family, I was always hoping and praying he would change and things would get better, but they never did. As it turns out, my daughter became my inspiration and the reason that I moved forward. She is the reason the divorce had to happen—I had to break the cycle for her so that she would not be exposed to childhood trauma. She was the reason that I was compelled to discover healing in my life. I needed so desperately for her to see something different than the narrative of darkness that consumed our home. I knew without question that I did not want her to be raised thinking that the emotional and psychological abuse that plagued our home was justifiable or acceptable. I needed to set the example for her to know that Love does not hurt, and when you feel like you are losing yourself, your spirit, and even your mind—it's time to go! I also recognized that my transition needed to happen amidst a very public presence in the beauty and entertainment industry. My job and business was and still is to present a face of hope and radiate the beauty of life in the face of public figures. My job and business is to make others look and feel more beautiful. Admittedly, this is not an easy feat, considering my personal life during that time was anything but beautiful. I didn't have the luxury of wallowing in despair, nor could I look like what I was going through. If I didn't move my brush or grow my business, I didn't eat or have the capacity to feed my child. Somehow, I channeled a strength that I had seen before—not only in my own mother, but in many single mothers who show up for their children, and I allowed it to motivate me. I couldn't go hide in a cave or give up a passion for beauty because I was going through trauma. This was not the answer. I was forced to face my beauty—my strength and self worth. There were days that I didn't know if I'd see my own light again. And on others, the ever-present glimmer of hope flickered in the distance. There are so many of us that have to push through publicly when no one knows the hell that we are suffering in private. Behind closed doors is a life and experience only the one's within the wall know about. In a healthy relationship, there is love and joy bouncing off the wall. When the relationship is toxic, it feels like sheer torture—from morning to night. I had to end it, I was dying inside, and if you've ever experienced that feeling, unfortunately you know it's slow and gradual, and then you begin to feel like you're losing yourself. Once that feeling started to set in, the reality of what my future self would look like after sacrificing of my worth, joy, and peace woke me up. I literally had to have that talk with myself: *Melissa, you don't deserve this, nor the baby. You don't deserve this...* In an instant, everything became clear.

𝒴 is for 𝒴ielding

THERE IS A SACRED SPACE THAT, WHEN CHANNELED, ALLOWS US TO DISCOVER OURSELVES OVER AND OVER AGAIN.

-MELISSA R. HIBBÉRT-

One of my greatest traumas occurred at a time in my life that I had envisioned would unfold so differently. My dreams of the white picket fence was shattered, and I found myself amidst a nightmare that seemingly would never allow me wake up. If I had learned nothing else from the trauma I experienced early in life, coupled with many hard lessons along the way, I learned that I was resilient. The ability to bounce back and to refuse to be overtaken by outside forces that would not serve as salve for my soul also meant that I had the power to overcome. And although the road ahead would prove to be arduous, I pushed my pen on the dotted line and filed for divorce when our daughter was only three months old.

THE LOOKING GLASS

Every face bears an untold story. We must take special care to note how we place judgement. No one would have known what I was going through had I never made the decision to disclose of my trauma. I heard the words of me "being fake" tossed around because those who knew a little about my situation expected me to run to social media to open up, but that wasn't my way.

I knew instinctively that it wouldn't be a smart move because, at the time, I had not done the processing or the healing. One day, a client of my came to town from Atlanta. She had several press events during her stay. During the makeup session, we were catching up. The conversation was lively and engaging as usual, but I remember feeling like I needed to go deeper—to open up. I shared with her that I would be filing for divorce. I shared with her a lot of the pain and trauma I had gone through. I also told her how tough the decision was and that I had no idea where I got the courage to walk away, after a year of marriage, with an infant in my arms. She looked at me and her response floored me. She said, "Baby girl, that was not courage—you are smart!" She went on to say, "It takes a smart person to see clearly that something isn't quite adding up. Those vows you made aren't quite being honored. Who he said he was is not who is showing up to be in your home. He's hurting you when he should be helping you." Through her words, it became clear: It's a smart thing to make the next right move for myself and our daughter—the decision to end the marriage. Her words soothed me and that was a healing moment. It was the extra confirmation for me. That I was moving in the right direction. I am a firm believer that we must all come to grips with the reconciliation of the events that take place in our lives to make sense of it all. There are times when we can't speak on the pain that we are experiencing because our voices have been compromised. This past year, I spent a great deal of time studying abuse, narcissistic personality disorder, and trauma. It became quite clear to me that the perpetrator's desire is to silence you—to make you feel unseen and unheard, to the world and even to yourself. There are many days where I can't believe this is my story, but the healed person in me knows that this was one of the greatest lessons I had to learn, the hardest road I had to travel, for a reason. I began to watch less reality tv and immersed myself in my own personal healing program that consisted of a lot of praying, reading, researching, studying, breathing, meditating forgiving, and listening. There was no existing "program" for my personal healing anywhere, so I created one, authentically to my own desire to get the lesson and be whole again. Once I became radical with my healing, it was easier for me to begin writing—starting with journaling my experiencing—all the way back from childhood to present day. I now believe that one of the greatest ways to heal is through transparency. This is the reason that I made the decision to share and reveal in this book. I knew I needed to heal, and I prayed daily that if God allowed me to use my life to inspire others in the process, then I would be forever grateful for that honor. I want so desperately to always do and say positive things, so to live such a negative experience shook me to my core—feeling the shame of failure was, and still is, hard to share. Growth has taught me, you can't heal what you don't acknowledge or reveal. One hard truth that I acquired is that healing is a personal choice, and it has to be a lifestyle.

It often angers me to hear people say negative things about women wearing wigs and makeup, often assuming they are doing it to mask who they really are. This simply is not true. The mere fact that we show up to sit in a chair or in front of a mirror to pull ourselves together speaks volumes. The mere fact that we choose to get out of bed to show up for the day proves that we are resilient. The alternative of the demonstration of resilience is laying in bed, popping pills, drinking alcohol, crying all day, hiding under the sheets with the lights out. We can opt to isolate ourselves and allow the pain to consume us, or we can opt to face the beauty that lives within. I have touched and transformed thousands of faces over the course of the years with my artistry, and I have heard many intimate stories—mostly painful and traumatic. I've had women ask me to cover up scars left behind from an abusive relationship. I've had women cry in my chair because they are finally doing something for themselves. And I have had women celebrating their makeup in the mirror with me when done but fearing what their husbands or boyfriends will say when they get home because it's their permission or validation that make them feel beautiful. For those of us who show up in spite of it all, I applaud relentlessly. It's harder to show up than it is to sit and be depressed and fall apart. Facing yourself in the mirror also means acknowledging truths that are uncomfortable. The truth for me was that I needed to have a better relationship with myself. In my healing, I discovered that I was weak with my boundaries—after all, I never learned how to set them. The people pleaser in me, the empath that I learned that I am, set the stage to be a target. How was I weak in my boundaries? I didn't speak up when I was treated badly. I made other's happiness my personal responsibility. I agreed to things I knew I was against, which led to self betrayal. Hindsight is twenty-twenty, and to face your beauty also means owning your stuff. I discovered that the more I began to peel back the layers, show up, and to give meaning to what I experienced and to stand firmly in my truth, the more power I had the potential to access within myself. We must never forget that showing up also means that the battle has already been won. Refuse to be hidden within yourself and the world. And when we feel that we are spiraling out of control or going into a depressive state, we gain clarity and composure by simply showing up.

I chose to acknowledge my experiences because I understood, after getting through this trauma, that I needed to master myself. Knowing my heart and understanding my internal compass is the only way that I would not be subjected to making the same mistakes again. Self-mastery is a profound experience. Even so, it is not an act that the world implies we engage in on a daily basis. No one wakes up thinking, "Today, I shall master myself." We wake up to consider mastering skills, jobs, art, sports, etc. After experiencing the whirlwind of going through a marriage, divorce, and transition into a single-mother in less than two years, I was left only with the obligation to know myself on a deeper level. And as smart as I know I am, amidst the degrees I've earned and the amazing experiences that I have been fortunate enough to realize, I ended up in a situation that was a clear result of missed signs. The red flags escaped me. I was living and attempting to thrive in a relationship that did not serve me so much so that even when things started falling apart, I was in a state of oblivion, forcing myself to take a step back, reflect and own it. Owning the moments that my gut was telling me something wasn't right, when life was speaking to me, and I didn't listen, when drama kept knocking, and I clearly had enough. I had the chance to say, "I am out," but instead I said, "I do." I regret nothing because I allowed my heart to lead the way. What I know now is that the heart and mind can thrive when in sync; mine were not. I also learned the importance of being "equally yoked," to have a partner who is on your team, ready to see you win, to add wind to your sail, and to love you actionably. For my healing, it became radical! Nothing was going to stop me from getting the lesson because I never, ever want to repeat it. Healing doesn't happen overnight. As I said, it is a lifestyle, and we should all take valued time to learn about ourselves and the internal motivations that we possess. Everything that is inside of us and even the things that happen to us, exists to teach us valuable lessons. It's all there to wake you up. In hindsight, I also recognize that many of my relationships were with the same type of person. The explanation for this became clear while living through this most traumatic time. The "Aha! moment" for me was during a therapy session where the counselor asked me to talk about my previous relationships in chronological order. The more I talked as she sat intently, the more I realized, I was attracting the same person, over and over again—he was just showing up in a different body, with a different name. Compromising moments of reflection deny us intuitiveness to rule out the people, places, and things that don't deserve to access our energy. Once I was committed to doing the work to master myself, the smoke cleared, and so many amazing revelations were given unto me. By doing this work and getting this far in my quest to master myself, I am now afforded an opportunity to guide my daughter—to teach her how to live in her light, set boundaries, and to honor herself first. I take great responsibility in knowing I have an opportunity, through my growth and healing, to elevate the generations that come after me. My mother still struggles to master herself. We have these types of conversations all the time. Even at sixty-nine years old, I find myself observing her during this process. Teaching my daughter to master herself also means that no one can rob her of her value and her right to be treated with actions worthy of her presence. For the rest of my days, my objective is to be true to me and to discover the power in honest assessments of myself. When I look in the mirror, I aspire to not only recognize who I see but to love her unconditionally. There is a voice inside each of us that doesn't quite learn to speak louder until we give it permission to do so. For me, this time is now.

TAKE ME TO THE KING

I would be remiss if I didn't speak about the spiritual connection that kept me sane during the moments that I was on the brink of falling. My relationship with God proved to be salve for my soul. And while I recognize that this might not be everyone's source, I am compelled to speak about mine. For me, it was God that allowed me to see that glimmer of light in the distance. I was raised to seek God first in all things. In reflection and the true spirit of evolution, I am reminded of many times in my marriage that I did not seek God first. I started off that way, but it was not how I ended. As our relationship went on, he really was not truthful about wanting a stronger relationship with God. There was always an excuse. I wanted us to go to church as a couple. I felt shameful walking into church solo when everyone knew I was in a relationship. The residue of the toxic behavior was a more prominent force in the relationship because we could never find our way to church—hate to sound cliche, but we only went on Mother's Day because it's tradition with his family. Although we had a faith-based foundation, the devil crept in and took over. I fell out of touch on a daily basis with my core guiding force. Life after the traumatic relationship has helped me to restore my faith, and I will never lose it again. No longer will I compromise my relationship with God for anyone. Recentering also meant reconnecting with the source and finding my way back to the things that I loved. Being born in Jamaica and residing in California, I am always amidst the lands of wind and water. I go to the beach more often and allow myself to feel. Choosing to heal in this way helped me to discover the necessity of doing something you love every day. If you do something you love everyday, it's fills the space that trauma once consumed.

YOU THINK YOU KNOW, YOU HAVE NO IDEA

After writing this book, both my heart and my mind continue to evolve. Transformative thinking and living has always come second nature to me by virtue of curiosity, but today, I desire to check in with myself more so now than ever. I just want to be free from anything that has the potential to weigh me down, hold me back, or steal my joy. I discovered freedom in understanding more of who I am. This current state has allowed me to see myself and the world around me with a different lens. I've also learned the art of sitting in complete silence; stillness is beautiful. Most recently, a quiet moment alone led me to a daydream that resonated with my soul. In that vision, I was on stage with Oprah. Yes, Oprah! I am imagining that I was there to discuss this book. As she sat up in her chair, she placed her hand under her chin and asked me two questions: "Why now? Why face your beauty? And what message do you hope readers will take away?" It was in that moment that I realized that I had been preparing for a time such as this for my entire life. The truth that my experiences both transformative and traumatic led me to is that I've been facing my beauty for my entire life. Admittedly, this has not always been by choice. In many instances, I faced my beauty because I had to. All that I have experienced has become the essence of who I was destined to be. When I close my eyes and allow myself to see with my soul, the way in which beauty is defined is completely altered. Beauty is not about what our eyes can see. Beauty is about our ability to discover the infinite Beauty—the essence of who we are. True Beauty is the essence of our being. Beauty is a divine gift that we are each born with that makes us whole and complete. Until we recognize that pain and trauma are proposed to rob us of our self image, innocence, worth, and divine grace, we will operate at a deficit when they show up at our doorstep, rather than seeing it as a sign ushering us towards our true self. And although we will not be exempt from pain or trauma, we will always have access to the transformative power of resilience because it is within each of us. Facing my beauty meant that I choose to face the fire and come out on the other side wearing a couture dress embezzled with flames. I have not allowed what I have been through to define me, nor will I. In the spirit of evolution, I have also recognized that the love that lives inside of me will never return void. There is no shame in journeying to rediscover that which has been stripped away. In these times, we must learn to celebrate finding victory in the fire. To face your beauty is to preserve your peace, protect your being, own your power, and to find your purpose—knowing you are always valuable, always worthy, and you are always enough.

AND I SHALL TELL THE WORLD

Knowing that you have been called to tell your story is one thing; moving forward in obedience to do so is another. It is my belief that we each have a chapter that is difficult to read or one that we don't desire for others to see. The decision to come forward with the truth rendered in this book came from the depths of my soul. In observation, it is possible that one might assume that my life has been a crystal stair. I choose to use my public platform as a haven for empowerment and to showcase the possibilities of what can be when we opt to follow our dreams without apology. Social media has risen to the top of the fray as a way to showcase our stories in ways unimaginable. As this is the case, everyone chooses to use social media very differently. If you look across the board at some of the most prominent people, they're not sharing their most intimate moments on public platforms. Many celebrities and influencers are not even showing their kids or families to the masses. Most of the time, what is showcased are moments that represent their brand. My sentiment is such that what I go through every day does not stop me from becoming the woman that I was destined to be. Emotional trauma does not define me; it happened to me. My platform of choice to be vulnerable and to give of myself was manifested while writing my truth in a way that it could never be erased or forgotten. The truth that lies within the pages of this book represents being the champion of my life. With my story and journey, I want the world to recognize that resilience is accessible to all. It is my hope to continue to construct a public platform that is vested in focusing on strength and courage (oh, don't forget being smart) while simultaneously writing and sharing my truths. It is my decision to focus on strength and courage, and that is the story that I shall tell the world. Looking back at my four-year-old self in Kingston, Jamaica, waiting for my mother to return while making the best of the cards life had dealt me, I was being prepared early. There is uncanny emotional profit in recognizing that our truths are to be given to the world in ways that will resonate infinitely. Let no one dictate how and when you decide to tell your story as long as you set your soul ablaze with the truth. Yielding to my own understanding was the bravest act that I have watched. In the end, yielding has been the essence of my transformation.

Being lost in darkness is the surest way to discover light.

-Melissa R. Hibbért-

Beautiful Faces: A Tribute to Untold Stories of Triumph

Camara's Journey

I'm originally from Brooklyn, NY. I've spent the past decade painting the world beautiful as a professional makeup artist. It brings me great joy to help my clients shine on red carpets and on the set of their films and TV shows. I've worked with so many amazing women and men, and I feel so blessed to share my gifts and talents in this capacity.

THE STORY

It is possible that we can trace many things that happen in our lives to their root causes. And while I am not saying that not having my father in my life is the root cause of the trauma that I experienced, I will say that his absence is a contributing factor. My first experience of emotional trauma was at the hands of the one who was divinely appointed to care for my heart. The lack of my father's presence was felt in many ways, but most profoundly in my inability to accept and acknowledge the red flags of danger in my relationships.

I can recall engaging in what would evolve into a seven-year relationship with a guy whom I was introduced to by a mutual friend. I was nineteen at the time. He was super sweet and, quite honestly, I felt like I'd found someone that I cared deeply about. We would talk on the phone all day and it was great. I later learned that he was dealing drugs to make ends meet. He wanted more for himself and attempted many times to create a different lane for himself. At that time, I was still trying to figure out who I was and what I wanted to do with my life. I had a few sources of income, and I did recognize that the world had more to offer than what was right in front of me. One of my sources of employment was modeling. This profession placed me front and center in the entertainment industry. I could tell that the presence of all of the celebrities and financial resources made him uncomfortable. If I had to guess, I would also say that he felt insecure about his finances in many ways. There were times my words didn't comfort him or silence his doubts. Admittedly, my attitude was not always the best, but it was most certainly not worthy of what I would be forced to endure.

I noticed a significant change in him after witnessing him curse his mother out. I could not believe the rage that he had towards the woman who sacrificed her life to birth him. It became apparent to me that if he didn't get his way with his family, he was capable of temper tantrums.

The magnitude of his insecurities continued to grow. He would often say, "I'm the man, and you have to respect me." Although I didn't understand what he was alluding to, I did consider that my lack of a father in my life could also mean that I didn't have all the answers as to how a man should be treated. I entertained the idea that I was out of touch with how to love in some ways.

There was an instance that I walked before him to get on the train and swiped my card first. My actions angered him so profusely that by the time we got on the train, he threw water in my face and embarrassed me in front of everyone.

That day, I got off and walked to a friends house and resolved that I was done. For whatever reason, I eventually came back. We would find ourselves in an on-and-off-again relationship that was ever evolving. I felt as though I had to constantly lift him up because he was so insecure. There were times that we would take the train and he would accuse a random guy of looking at me. He would get so angry that he would attempt to strike up a fight. In many instances, the passenger whom he targeted would state that they were simply reading the signs or, more importantly, not even looking in our direction.

I always felt like I was walking on eggshells in his presence. He would often get angry for no reason or go through my phone in a rage at the prospect of discovering some indiscretion that didn't exist. There were times that he put his hands on me. He would grab me and throw me against the gate in anger. There were so many times that I blamed myself because he knew how to manipulate me back into a happy place. After a bout or an argument, he would do something sweet like send flowers. My grandmother would say, "Well, he sent flowers. Maybe you should give him another chance." Her words resonated with me. One Valentine's Day, he rolled out the red carpet for me. He bought tickets to see my favorite singer, gifted me a dress and shoes, and spent a ton of money on our excursion. We stayed in the dream hotel, went to the spa, and it was without question that I was in the presence of the guy who I had fallen for. The moments like this made me believe that no one else would love me the way that he had. I honestly thought that I would not ever find better.

His inconsistent working situation also meant that he was living with me in my apartment. Although he needed to live with me, it also frustrated him because he believed that the man should be recognized as the financial breadwinner, even though he wasn't doing so.

As time went on, he began to express that he wanted to have a baby together. His wish was granted shortly after I became pregnant. He had been working diligently to get his illegal activity back off the ground, but to no avail. My pregnancy became the most obvious factor for him to place the blame. It was almost as if he saw my pregnancy as a reason that stood in the way of his lack of success.

I can remember him attending one of my doctor's appointments to see the sonogram. He was two hours late, and when he arrived, there was no remorse. "You need to be okay with the fact that I'm fucking here. I'm here, but I didn't want to fucking come," he exclaimed. That day, even the doctor expressed her concern for my going forward with the pregnancy. In her office, she sat me down and asked, "Are you sure that you want to do this?" I confirmed that I was sure I wanted to move forward. A week later, things went from bad to worse. His anger had turned violently physical. He hit me in the back of my head and the force knocked me to the ground. I fell on my stomach and he began dragging me back into the apartment and proceeded to choke me and put a pillow over my face. I was yelling and screaming, "He is trying to hurt me. I'm pregnant. Stop!" My heart was crushed when no one even opened their door to acknowledge the undeniable screams. I calmed down to protect the baby and he stopped attacking me. I resolved that I wanted nothing more to do with him in any way shape or form, and I left never to return.

Hurt, in despair, and traumatized, I made the decision to have an abortion. It was all I knew to do to ensure that I never had to engage with him ever again. This moment was a devastating time for me. I questioned if I had made the right decision on so many occasions. The only thing that I was certain of was the fact that I could not have a baby with him. The relationship and the decision had been so traumatizing to me that I went into a state of denial. I would tell people that I *lost* the baby. I also harbored anger that I didn't know how to channel. No one understood the depth of my pain and loneliness. No one knew that he took all of the money that I had saved to pay bills while I was out with the baby. No one realized that I had to return to work immediately after having the abortion. I literally had to go back to work while still appearing physically pregnant. The trauma led me down a path that made me very numb to emotions in general. I found solace in not feeling. I dealt with so much in silence. My family did check on me and spend time with me and share their personal stories with me, but those whom I had called friends were nowhere to be found.

I do believe that time heals us in ways that immediate gratification cannot. The more I went to work, saved my money, and focused my attention toward healing, the more thing shifted.

I was blessed to have a landlord who supported my transition and allowed me to break my lease without penalty. I was on the road to healing, but it most certainly was not easy. Eventually, life led me into the arms of someone who desired to help and not harm me. The new guy that I began dating was nothing short of amazing. Life is a funny teacher at times. The past has a way of playing a joke in which it calls your name in the distance. The question always becomes, *Will you answer?* One day, my ex called to tell me that his father died. I dropped everything that was happening in the relationship that was serving me well to go and be by his side. Needless to say, the relationship that I had taken for granted ended, and I loved and lost.

THE LESSON: THE RELATIONSHIP WITH GOD MUST ALWAYS BE GREATER

Losing someone who was amazing while opening the door that had already been closed by God was a hard lesson. It took enduring this tumultuous time in my life to ensure that I would never return to anything that no longer served me, or that God had not sent. I do believe that not having seen a father figure, and the encouragement from my family to go back when apologies were made, encouraged me to consider if I was justified in leaving many times. But we must learn that it is only the conviction of God that we should be in search of. This journey has taught me to sit still and be quiet to hear what God is asking me to do. I have not been in a relationship for over eight years. If I see anything that triggers my thoughts of the past traumatic experiences, I immediately remove myself. In this season, my relationship with God has been strengthened. Today, I am focusing on hearing

God. I have even had someone to prophesy over me. I believe with all my heart that God always speaks through others. I was told that everything I had been through was exclusively for my testimony. If I had not gone through the traumatic moments, I would not be the kind of woman that I am today. Grace is so wondrous, and favor is such a blessing. The most profound words that the pastor spoke to me are still in my heart: "You will no longer attract abusive relationships or people that want to hurt you." Today, I am attracting real love, real friendships, and the real meaning for my life.

My goal from this point forward is to search for ways to help others to find the beauty in their lives.

Dunnie's Journey

I am a full time visual studio artist. I am also a muralist who enjoys painting on canvas and walls. I have my own studio in the D.C. metro area. When I am not painting, I inspire my audience as a social media influencer. I also execute branding for fashion lines and model.

THE STORY

I was raised in Maryland surrounded by the love of my mother and father, but after attending college in Alabama, I was extended a job offer in LA. Although I was elated, I had no family or friends when I arrived and, subliminally, I'm certain that I was open and looking to connect with people. One day, I decided to go to Trader Joe's to pick up a few items. I was approached by a gentleman, and we stood in the aisle and talked casually. At the end of our exchange, he asked if I would allow him to contact me again. We talked a little more and then I provided him with my business card.

Several days went by and I didn't hear from him. For me, it was out of sight, out of mind.

Approximately a week or so later, he reached out, and it was apparent that he was interested in us hanging out. We decided to go on our first outing together and things were cool. We engaged in the normal exchange of information about one another, which led to a brief discussion about attending college. I shared that

Tuskegee University is my alma mater. He responded in kind and shared with me that he was an alumni of Virginia State. He also told me that he did not have any children which was significant to me because if we decided to go further in our relationship, there would be no other parties involved. We enjoyed each other's company and had a second date shortly thereafter.

The more time that we spent together, the more I learned about who he was and his character. I learned that he had several run-ins with the law. He assured me that there was nothing that I should be concerned about.

Our relationship moved forward relatively fast. We decided to get engaged and even began building a business from the ground up together. Our world was on autopilot, and the life that I had once imagined for myself was morphing into a reality. The cultivation of our business and our family was in full swing, and then came a baby. I believe with my whole heart that our conception was a sign from God about our relationship and a beacon of hope for me to put my reservations to bed. Even though I had been skeptical, I wanted to believe that the baby and the direction that we were heading in was in the best interest of our growing family.

The drug use (marijuana) ensued, and his display of paranoia went from subtle to glaring. To add insult to injury, he also started taking pills. When I questioned him, he would tell me that he was taking vitamins and that I didn't know what I was talking about.

I no longer felt safe in the home that we had created together. I stored many of my belongings at a friend's place and made the excruciating decision to move back to Maryland to give birth to my daughter. I wanted to have the support of my family and to feel at peace during this life transition. I knew that doing so was the best thing for me and my daughter at the time, but it was hard. A long-distance relationship was not what he wanted, but he was left with no other choice. I remained in Maryland after having our daughter.

By the time she turned one, he was flying back and forth a great deal. I knew he hated it. We had been working to repair the things that had been broken in our relationship, so I resolved to go back to LA to try once more for the family. I had grown up with both of my parents in my home, and I wanted the same for my daughter.

When we returned, it became apparent to me just how much drug use and addiction had become a part of his daily routine. Even still, I was not even aware of the extent that his usage was progressing. Things went from bad to worse when we became homeless. It seemed as though I was the only one working to ensure that the business stayed afloat; it was our financial lifeline. He didn't want to put forth the effort and energy to ensure that his family had a place to live. He chose his drug use over our well being. I was extremely stressed out. Not only did his drug usage come to light, but so did the fact that he was not who he professed to be. He eventually came clean about not having gone to college. It was almost as if I was living with a complete stranger. The thought of it frightened me. Concerned that I was not raising my daughter in an environment conducive to her wellbeing, I made the decision to leave again. This time, I resolved to walk away from it all. I even let go of the business, which was one of the most hurtful things that I had to come to terms with. So many people questioned how I could let go of something that I had worked so hard to construct. I didn't have the answers back then. What I did know was that I had to rid myself of the toxic environment and protect my daughter.

When I filed for divorce, all I ever demanded was freedom. I didn't ask for alimony, child support, the furniture, or the resources. Only freedom. And although I was free from his wrath physically, he embarked upon a heinous journey to hurt me in other ways.

Out of spite, he took our company's business page and deleted all of the images that had generated income over the years and turned it into his personal account. He launched a smear campaign by posting memes about me and my family. He would go live on Instagram and tell the world that I used him to have a baby and other derogatory things about my family. I began receiving unsolicited messages telling me that I was a terrible person and questioning why I took a child away from a father who wanted to be present. They had no idea of the personal hell that I was experiencing in the moments not shared on social media. I lost an incredible amount of followers, and our swimwear company tanked, which also meant that there was no income. I returned home to Maryland with no finances, no business, and a tattered sense of self. I had to start over. I can recall my parents asking me what I would do for money. I had been doing some consulting work behind the scenes, so I leveraged some of my business relationships to get back into the fashion space. Emotionally, I recognized that I needed an outlet to channel the misplaced feelings of all of the trauma that I had experienced. I decided to go to the craft store and pick up some paints and brushes and canvases. One day, I took those supplies out into my parents' garage, and I allowed the brush to flow. It was as if God was guiding my hands. Painting became a spiritual experience for me and one that I so desperately needed. I started sharing my creations on my social media account, and they were met with positive feedback. Painting changed my life and ushered in a new era of purpose.

THE LESSON: GOD'S GRACE IS SUFFICIENT

As a result of pouring into my creations, I was able to build a strong enough body of work to apply for a studio artist program at an art gallery. Today I am a studio artist full time. I am exhibiting my work and receiving commissions for a gift that I never even received formal training to do. Creativity on this level, and the purpose that was embedded deep within, could never have surfaced while in the presence of disarray. God needed to isolate me and teach me how to discover peaceful pastures within myself.

I had an artist talk recently, and I shared some of my story. It is my hope to continue to share it so that it might positively impact someone else who may be facing similar circumstances. Today, I am aligned and in my purpose. I can say with the fullness of conviction that no man created an opportunity for me. Today, my daughter is thriving and surrounded by love. All of the credit for what has not manifested in my life can only be attributed to God's grace.

Katina's Journey

I was born in Seattle and raised in Portland. I am an interior architect by trade. In 2015, my creativity empowered me to develop a leather and exotic handbag line. Today, I specialize in fashion and interior design.

THE STORY

I would venture to say that I had a rough childhood. My father was in the military, and he was abusive to my mother. Growing up, I recognized that she had some severe issues. She had a rough upbringing and was placed in boarding school, which likely contributed to who she eventually became. She had even witnessed her mother taking her own life. I think that it affected her in ways unimaginable. Even though I know she loved me, I'm not sure if she knew the best way to raise me. I was in and out of various homes and, by my senior year, I was completely responsible for myself. All of these factors and more would eventually contribute to who I chose to embark upon a relationship with and my experiences.

As an adult, I can remember attending an intimate concert with my best friend at the time. She invited one of her guy friends, which was not out of the ordinary. We all hung out together, and I caught him looking at me a few times, but I thought nothing of it. She told me soon thereafter that he asked for my number. She refused to give it to him because I was in a place where I was not in search of a relationship. Over the next few weeks, he attempted to get me to go on a date with him through communication with her, to no avail. I was laser-focused on my business. After continuous prodding and encouragement from her, I decided to go on a date with him. At first consideration, he seemed really cool. I was intrigued by his intelligence. He did not take me to fancy restaurants, but I knew he had the capacity to do so. I often wondered if he was testing me to learn more about my character. Even though we talked a lot, he didn't ask me a lot of personal questions. I was in a space where I thought that I was a train wreck emotionally, so the less prodding, the better. I was used to beating myself up for so many reasons, but I was not standing amidst judgement with him. Him not asking me a lot of questions helped me to see that we were able to enjoy each other's company with no real strings attached. After he asked me to attend church with him, I began to open up more. I felt like I had been exposed to another side of him, and I became comfortable. Even after several interactions, he never came into my home (and I never went into his). We had unspoken boundaries. We must have gone on at least twenty dates prior to even discussing next steps in our relationship.

One Christmas, I found myself somewhat depressed, as the holidays often spark a hint of sadness for me. I vowed to spend quality time with my godmother, and I left my phone unattended. After a few days had gone by, I called him. His response shocked me. He told me that he felt as though we were not totally connected and that bothered him. He expressed his desire to make our relationship exclusive.

We connected on so many levels. He was a serial entrepreneur, and so was I. He built million dollar homes, and I designed million dollar homes. He sold eighteen wheelers to people and had also done a lot of import and export ventures. He always had great ideas, and I respected his professional opinion. I began to place him on a pedestal in many ways. He had big thoughts and big ideas. I'm a big thinker too, but I'm also detail-oriented. Our discussions led us towards the things that we could do together. He was also very instrumental in coaching me through business scenarios that did not serve me. I ran into an encounter where one of my clients refused to pay me for a massive job that I had expounded great pride, resources, and energy towards. It was an extremely stressful time, and I had to go to court to get the matter resolved. I was emotionally connected to my projects more than money, I wanted everything to be beautiful for my clients. I wanted everyone to be happy and at peace with the work I created. He was so supportive and encouraged me to venture out even more with my business. "You should start your own home textiles line," he said. I was wondering how an act of this magnitude could be accomplished at the time. He reassured me by saying, "I've done manufacturing overseas for years, and I can take you over to show you how it's done." All I knew was that I had prayed for a relationship that would allow me to build with someone, and it appeared to be unfolding right before my eyes. He kept his word and there we were, on foreign soil discussing tanneries and textiles. I was inspired by the possibilities, but also guided by practicality. Upon our return, I recognized that doing a home textiles line was not as easy as it appeared. After careful observation, I came to recognize that businesses of this nature do well when people are famous or when they represent more well-known brands. I did however recognize that everyone wore handbags in every country we traveled to. It was in this realm of creativity that the handbags line came to fruition. He had introduced me to a whole new world, and I ran full speed ahead towards destiny. As we continued to evolve as a couple, we shared many similarities and many differences. It became apparent that our work ethics matched, which was beneficial to the attainment of our goals. He was very frugal and managed his money well. He had also been manufacturing shoes overseas and selling them in the U.S. The difference between us was that he had a "pop the trunk" mentality. I knew immediately that this was not the sentiment that I wanted to surround my brand. I wanted to establish a luxury brand. And even though there were things that we didn't necessarily see eye to eye on, I made the decision to go all the way in and give the relationship my all.

I began moving full speed ahead to learn the new industry. I was even learning to communicate in different languages! Our relationship was flourishing. Eventually, we became pregnant. He was so excited about the new life we had created together. I felt like God had given me everything I asked for. Although I had promised myself that I would never move in with someone that I was in a relationship with until after being married, the prospect of creating a family together caused me to rethink my decision. Shortly after moving in to his home, we lost the baby.

With a broken heart, I resolved to pour myself and my pain into creating the handbag line. When it was launched, he was extremely supportive. I shared with him that I wanted to name the company something that symbolized us and the relationship that we shared. He was not in agreeance with that choice. He encouraged me to be the face of the brand. A partnership evolved when I did a big design job with a PR firm in exchange for PR services. At the time, I didn't have the capital to pay outright; but I had my talent, and that was a treasure. When the company began to flourish and the PR firm began to cultivate the campaign, he became different. I can recall one evening him asking, "Well what about me?" I panicked and reminded him of how he had declined being involved. I also reassured him that I was determined to work with the company to recreate the strategy to include him. He declined, but I could tell he was dissatisfied. As sales began coming through for the business, his demeanor shifted. It hurt me deeply to hear him say, "You got it now. I'm done." He invested some money to get us started, and he shared knowledge. I took the knowledge he shared and ran with it, but I also knew that the brand needed finances to reach our goals. This also meant that I would need to work hard to take the company to the next level. It had been my understanding that he supported this decision, but his actions sang a different song.

After careful consideration, I recognized that the handbag line was not going to survive without financial backing. I looked to him for support. I took the time to craft a detailed financial statement and requested to meet in public so that we would not have an argument and remain focused on business. I showed him what was needed to sustain the business in hopes of garnering his contribution. His response shocked me: "I don't give a fuck if I ever put another dollar into this. I'm getting 50 percent no matter what." Right then and there, I asked him, "Do you want the handbag line or the relationship?" "I don't want anything if I can't have both," he replied. That was the last straw for me, and I made the decision to relocate to NY. There I began working on a business plan of my own. It was as if he was stalking me because he would know about various moments and events happening in my life even though I was not in contact with him. He would even be aware of times when I was working on some significant contracts. He would call me and say things like, "You can't do anything for this business without me." I even discovered that he had been spying on me through my Dropbox account for the whole year after my departure and our breakup.

As fate would have it, Marriott acquired Starwood, and my contract in NY had come to an end. Before making a decision about what I would do next, I recommitted my entire being to God and prayed and asked for guidance about everything. I had maintained my condo in Atlanta, and I was offered another position with Marriott once I returned home to Atlanta. When I arrived, I laid on my face, and God told me to wait. I did not accept the role in accordance with God's directive. I must have remained in waiting for approximately a year. During that time, I was still fighting to get over the trauma that I had experienced in the relationship. He would reach out to me from time to time, reminding me of his presence. That made it much harder for me. I saw from afar that he was developing many new business ventures, and it was surprising to me because he had made me feel that he did not have the resources to invest in the venture that we had once believed in together.

God sent me an angel who encouraged me to move forward with the development of the handbag line and to seek trademark rights. Eventually, I came to the realization that I had not signed anything with my ex, and the chains of bondage that I held myself with were not real. I began to pray for protection over the gift and creativity that God placed in me. He had two years to do take the business idea and run with it, but he hadn't. My goal became to align with whatever God had in store for me and to never look back. I resolved to be totally celibate and to do anything that would bring me closer to God. Choosing God's direction for my life allowed me to silence the negative words that had once proven to be powerful in my life but no longer.

The Lesson: True Joy and Real Peace is Priceless

I recently had a call for a potential contract for a 5.5 million dollar boutique hotel for my business. The things that are coming to me now that I have allowed God into my heart are beyond my wildest imagination. I have had the honor and privilege to experience joy in its purest form. This joy that I speak of is not because my money is long; it is because I am free. Although I am not in a committed relationship, I'm not lonely. I am not sad. My mind is no longer abusing me. I have learned to enjoy moments of serenity and silence and my own company. The most important lesson that I have learned through the trauma and through the pain is that true beauty is in the palm of God's hands. Today, my faith is my first priority, and I am so in love with the journey.

Sandye's Journey

My name is Sandye Lomax. I was born and raised in Baltimore, Maryland. I am the oldest girl of three brothers. I grew up between Baltimore City and Glen Burnie. I'm kind of a well-rounded person in a lot of different ways. I have no kids. I will be forty-seven in April. I became a disability specialist and worked for the city of Baltimore for fifteen years. I had gotten into a relationship that I ended up moving to New Jersey for. I took a leave of absence, and I got a little lost of myself, and I tried to figure out what I wanted to do. I asked myself what would I do for free in life. I wanted to make people feel beautiful and good about themselves. I decided to go and get a cosmetology license, a nail technician license, and train in eyelash extensions. I have my own business called Beauty Fetish, and I feel like the name is an umbrella of all the things I like to do as it relates to beauty. When my grandmother was passing from cancer, I noticed that the one thing that made her feel good was combing her hair, putting a little lipstick on, and polishing her nails. I just wanted people to feel that every day. I feel rewarded enhancing outer beauty. But most of all, I believe true beauty starts within.

THE STORY

When I look back over my dating history, I realize I've gone through it many times. I just wasn't aware of what I was experiencing. In the early stages, I was introduced to a guy through a mutual friend. The mutual friend was married, so I trusted his judgement. Him and his wife were good friends of mine. When I met the guy, it was supposed to be business, but with the intention that he was secretly trying to connect me with someone. I went over to talk about redecorating his house, and we just got to talking. He had a beautiful home. His kids looked well-groomed. I found out he had been married for twenty-three years. Everything seemed perfect about him. He even owned his own auto-shop. He was a grown man, had groomed kids, spoke well, had a beautiful home, owned business, AND had a hobby. I had learned from experience that when you strip a man of his work and power, they don't know what they like to do, so it was nice to see he had a hobby. He knew what he liked to do, and he had money set aside. I thought he was such a great guy. I got sick one day, and he offered to bring me soup. Something went wrong with my car, and he offered to look at it. He was the perfect gentleman. The first date was on his birthday. I decided to treat him to dinner. Six months after meeting his kids, I knew they really liked me, and I liked them. He told me he wanted to be with me. We got intimate. I ended up getting pregnant. I've only had miscarriages, so I was unsure. But, he knew what he wanted, and he went out and got a ring. I was so excited. About six weeks into the pregnancy, I had a miscarriage. I remember when I had the miscarriage, we were walking around the house talking. He was talking in circles and finally started talking about some girl he was talking to not knowing he had a baby on the way, da da da. He just kept talking really fast. And I told him, "Hold up. What?" And he said, "Well, I don't know. When I was between marriages, there was a one-night stand, and now the girl is saying she's pregnant." I was devastated. Here I was, still bleeding out what's left of our child, and he's having a child with someone else. I felt like a truck had come out of nowhere and hit me. Why wouldn't he tell me this when he met me? That would've changed the whole dynamic of our relationship. I don't even know if I would've gotten involved with him. And he said, "Well, I didn't know if it was mine." There were so many lies, I didn't know what to believe. Here I was thinking he was a good guy, and my friends were saying, "Well maybe he got scared, or he was really hoping it wasn't his." I remember sitting at home still resting, while he went to North Carolina. The day he was getting tested was when she was delivering a baby boy and, lo and behold, it was his. I was devastated. At that age, I hadn't had any of my own kids, and I didn't want to raise anyone else's. I felt like that had been snatched from me. That was the early stage.

After that, I believed him. Maybe he did just have a one-night stand, and it happened before me. It wasn't like he cheated on me. I believed everything he said. Maybe God said, "You can't have kids, but I'll give you the opportunity to help raise one." That was the first red flag I ignored. As time went on, I found out that he was still seeing the young lady here and there. He was saying he was confused, and he was going to New Orleans to visit his mother's grave. A woman's intuition gave me an eerie feeling saying something wasn't quite right. I went on the young lady's Facebook page and saw that she was in Las Vegas. Then one of his friends told me because she saw that this girl was getting swindled, and she had no idea who she's really dealing with. He was in Las Vegas with her. I had thought he was visiting his mother's grave and getting his mind right. All these red flags came along. When he found out I knew he was with her, he left Las Vegas and came home. Then I found out the diamond ring he gave me wasn't real. All these things started happening. I started feeling sorry for him. I found out he was adopted. Everyone in the whole town he grew up in knew but him. I thought maybe he had resentment towards women. He said he would go to counseling because he loved me. And I mentally started falling for the lies and manipulation. If I went out again, would I find someone else who had a kid and wouldn't tell me?

As things progressed, I found out more lies. His auto-shop was in a location that wasn't the best. I was thinking how could help him grow. I could help him get rid of his big computer. I'd get him some business cards made, or I'd talk to him about taking a car and donating it to a woman with a child instead of junking it. It'd be nice to fix it up and help somebody. I had all these lovely ideas about how to help him grow, but never about how I could help myself grow. All the things he made me believe were broken. The deception slipped through the cracks in the little things: I would be at work getting emails during the day or scrolling on my Facebook pages and uncover yet another lie. I never knew that it was a revolving door of women after women. And nothing impressed me. Nothing impressed me in cars or money. I found out that not only did I not have his baby, but his baby mama was in her twenties. He was in his forties. Why would he put me through this? When I found out he was in Las Vegas and he left the young lady there, he professed his love for me and had friends and his kids get involved. It took some time, but I forgave him. I thought that maybe I got a good one, and I just needed to work with him. He pulled off multiple lives without anyone knowing. We ended up moving in together. All of the, "I love you. I want to marry you," was a farce. There were other scorned women showing up and scratching his truck up and leaving notes. He said he was going to counseling. We joined church together because he wanted to change. It was all manipulation. He never was going to change. He made me believe he was going to change. It was a total scam played out to the T. Later I found out he was going through a lot of different chicks. There was one girl he would go out of town with. I thought he was going out of town on business, but he was just going out with her.

It was a masterful manipulation that never stopped. I was so afraid to get out because what if I found someone else just like that? I'm a nourisher. We want to fix and help. You find yourself torn. It was just all a game. I found out about a young lady he had been seeing. He was using her. She thought that she was going to get an airport auto-shop deal, but it was all fraud. Basically, she didn't get the deal, he dropped her, and he said that he was going to counseling. I looked up who he said he was getting counseling from. She looked like she would get it. I actually went in to see her and mentioned that he had referred me. She asked if I would be interested in couple's counseling. I said, "No, I've been through hell and back," One time, he was so delirious he handed me his phone. I remember his phone rang and it said Mercedes on it. Our counselor. And I thought, "Weird, Mercedes wouldn't be open this late." So, I answered and said hello. And she asked if so and so was available. I said, "No, we're having a family crisis. Can I have him call you back?" She said, "Family crisis???" I said, "Yes, I'm his fiancé. I can have him call you back later." She told me how they had just had sex before going to the Bahamas and that he loved her and wanted to meet her kids. I had no idea. I work in a room with clients all day, so I had no idea that he could see the same movie we saw in the evening with her during the day. He made me go through the phone, and I found eleven chicks who were being told the same thing: Dave and Buster's waitresses, anyone that made him feel above and better. So, I was devastated to find out that this person who seemed like an amazing guy turned out to be the opposite. I went to the counselor. She said he didn't want to see her anymore, but that before she went, she had him sign a form. She tricked him into signing a form that allowed her to talk about everything with me. She diagnosed him as a sociopath. She told me I should get a restraining order right away because he is dangerous. This is what he does to women. She's telling me all of this, and I'm just in shock. She's telling me about some other young lady he's seeing and how he was trying to manipulate her into giving him money. The manipulation had been nonstop to the point that I thought I was going crazy. I spent many nights and days thinking I was losing my mind. I spent many nights feeling torn and trying to figure out what I should do. Every time when I started drifting away, he would show up. He just played on it. He would show up ringing my doorbell, coming into my house. Sometimes there would be really nasty messages, then a few hours later, he would he say, "You don't understand how much I love you." It was an emotional rollercoaster ride. I literally just wanted to die. I wouldn't have done anything to actually kill myself, but how could I see past the lies when someone seems so sincere, so warm? You spend hours with them every day, but they're living multiple lives. How do you get past this? I went and saw the counselor. She had me come in twice a week. I had to sit in front of him and ask why he did this to me.

The day his dad passed, he had a lot of resentment. I went to New Orleans with him to bury his dad. I remember on his Instagram, a lady said on his post, "He is so strong. He lost his dad and his baby this week." Now there was another chick with another baby on top of the other lady with the other baby? I didn't understand how he had all this time to live these lives.

I learned a lot about myself through counseling. I went despite the stigma in the black community for going to get help. I told her things I never told anyone before about being raped and being the oldest girl among boys. I lived in a Catholic family, and I never wanted to break my family up. So, during counseling, I found out a lot about myself and why he was able to manipulate me and tell me so many lies. He was even able to get me hooked on his children. Children can pick up traits, and they become manipulative without meaning to. They just fell for me because I was the one that stuck around and making sure they had Christmases and birthdays. I wanted to hold on to what seemed secure. It was eye-opening to me. I sat him down and asked why he did this to women. He said he stopped going to the one counselor because she was best friends with the one lady I find out about. So here was a woman that I trusted and telling everything to and thinking I'm getting help, when at the start she was telling me to get a restraining order because she was upset by what he had done to her girlfriend. Then I was devastated because I felt like I've been manipulated by everybody. I went to the counselor, and I asked her if she was friends with this lady.

She replied, "Well it's one of degree separation here." But by then, I had researched her Facebook page and saw that we had mutual friends. There were just so many events. There was another time when he said there was a fire and that he was bringing her clothes and blankets. Eventually I found out that he couldn't see the fire at the barbershop like he said he did. He was actually sleeping with her, and they knocked over a candle. It's so detailed you don't have any reason not to believe until you find out.

I don't think I ever made it over. I think I made it through. It ripped a piece of me out that I don't think I will ever be able to put back in. It makes me want to help other women not to ignore the red flags. I didn't know what sociopath meant until I researched it. Sociopaths are narcissists. I missed so many of the signs. Everything was about him, him, him. I missed that sign. I didn't pay attention to it. I continued to stroke his ego. I went through a really, really depressed state. The one thing about me is I'm a relationship person. I love family. I'm in Atlanta alone. I have a cousin that is married and lives far out. I never pictured being almost forty-seven with no kids and being alone. As much as I love myself and I love my me time, I am missing a partner, a companion. I'm just learning to try to open up and trust, which is difficult because I realized I went through the same pattern. There was a pastor that reached out to me, and I fell for it again. I fell for believing. Everyone sees him as an amazing and inspiring mega pastor. He told me he was going through a divorce. Little do they know, he's a liar. I thought that he had no reason to lie. Then bam, you look up, and there's no divorce. They're a happy family. It's something I attract. I have learned that I am broken. Now I'm trying to figure out how to attract something different. People say you attract what you are. I do believe I attract broken people, but I have a warm spirit. I attract manipulative people. They're attracted to me because they know I give or that I believe in the manipulation. Sometimes it's people not wanting to maliciously hurt me, but looking for someone that will heal them in the moment. And that's why I get hurt. I'm still getting over it. I want to date, but I don't know where to begin. I'm trying not to put the past on anyone new. I think that's a way of protecting me. I accept that I will never have kids. I wonder if I would be a parent that would constantly worry if they would run into what I have run into. They're safe. I'm still getting over it. It's still a part of my healing process.

I'm trying to figure out how to heal day by day. I engulf myself in work trying to build my brand and my business. Trying to stay busy, to keep moving, and clear my head. Sometimes it plays with everything that I have experienced. When I think about it, I'm not really doing anything in particular now because I don't trust counseling. To actually go to a counselor and tell some of my deepest darkest family secrets and find out that this person was manipulating me as well, was devastating. I'm at a place where I don't know what to do for myself. This is probably why I'm choosing to share my story. I do have amazing friends and an amazing support system. I try to stay positive. I look at all the negative things now and wonder how to make sense of it all. The turmoil it took me through. The mental and physical and the humiliation. It's so deep, it's hard to pull it all out. If I had to say what I'm doing for myself, it's sharing it and speaking it out loud, which is giving me a sense of healing. I'm being bold about it and being courageous about it saying this is what happened to me. This is not to play the victim, but to understand where I went wrong and how I ignored things I shouldn't have. Now when I see a red flag, I immediately turn away. I don't play mental games with myself or fix the person, whether that be a friend or a romantic partner. It's a deal breaker. I keep it moving. There is no in between at this point. I'm being more aware, more alert, and sharing. What I went through is paying it forward. That's how it makes sense to me. You had to go through it, so you could share it and maybe let someone else understand what they're going through. A lot of times, when you're going through it, you don't understand what it is. Especially for women. We are nourishers. We want to fix. We want to believe, we want hope. The older we get, the lonelier we get when we can't find the perfect person. We go into it knowing that no one is perfect, but what are our deal breakers. What can't I ignore? Now I just reek positive quotes and keep a positive attitude.

THE LESSON: LOVE YOURSELF FIRST

When you love yourself the way that you deserve to be loved, you aren't tempted to accept manipulation. You can see it, and you love yourself so much that you're gonna recognize a red flag and learn from the stories that have been shared. And as soon as you see a red flag, you're going to go in the opposite direction. That would be my advice. I didn't have anyone to share stories with me or give me advice. We watch social media and hear about relationships, but I hadn't had a conversation with someone that went through it. I had no direction through it. I didn't have a spiritual grounding. I didn't know if God was telling me to work with this person, or if God was telling me leave. I have shown you every possible sign to leave. You cannot fix this person. You go and worry about yourself. Always put yourself first. You have to love yourself to say enough is enough. You have to try, and you have to believe. You can't go into a situation not believing. You have to give people the benefit of the doubt, otherwise you might miss out on the right one. You have to go out and try. But immediately when you see the lies, the manipulation, the blame, the inability to take accountability for their actions, you need to walk away before you're sucked in because they will destroy you. I'm glad I was strong enough to survive the things I went through. If you see the red flags, go in the other direction.

It's so tough. I work with women, and I hear the stories all day long. Until I started talking about it, I really thought it was just me. It's healing. With my clients, I can't talk about it, and I can't give them advice because it's a professional setting. The conversation is limited, but it's about them sharing with me. All day long they dump on me. So, I have to figure out how I can share their stories. I kept hearing these stories of cancer surviving and so many different things. Now to have a platform to share my story is so helpful. It pulls up emotions you forgot you still had and pain you were still holding in. What I learned is mental manipulation is a dangerous thing. The mind can be a weak playground to play on. I felt like the pastor was a predator because he had already followed me on social media. All the things he told me about he only knew because he had seen my page. He knew I was a family-oriented person. It goes back to the beginning. He's a predator. He preyed on me knowing I was a good-hearted person. I hate that these people who are narcissists and mental manipulators don't care or don't realize how bad they can tear a person up and affect their lives permanently. There will always be those little pieces of doubt if they're telling the truth about going to the grocery store. They can make you believe on a rainy day that the sky is shining and beautiful. They're just so good at it. I just don't know. I wish there was a way for manipulators to know what they're doing so they can understand the magnitude of damage they're doing. Like with the pastor who was preying on good-hearted women besides me. Why lie? Why be manipulative? It's their sickness. You are a victim, but you also have to recognize how you let yourself down or how you didn't see this. Or if you saw this, why did you continue? Why did you play into this? Now I'm in a place where I love me. I won't settle for less than. I know I won't meet anyone perfect, but I don't want to be alone all my life. I want a healthy relationship. I have to figure out the necessary steps to continue to heal. If there are healthy options to healing, whether it's a counselor or something else used for good, that makes me feel good.

It's not until we have a dialogue with each other and we're open that we realize so many of us go through this. Life keeps moving. As women, we just pick up the pieces and keep moving.

You can survive it with a smile and look good too.

Keith's Journey

I'm a filmmaker who specializes in post production in New York City. This is my second career, so it's been about ten years professionally. Before that, I was in the music business in New York City.

I mean, for me, I'm extremely familiar with this abuse stuff. Most of my relationships have been toxic.

THE STORY

I met her and I chased her. I took it really slow (or at least I tried to take it slow) since I just got out of a relationship. We would hang out, go on dates, and such. I didn't kiss her for three months, and she was like, "Why didn't you kiss me?" I was just feeling like a fish out of the water.

When I met her, I was working at a bar. She came in with her friends, and I noticed how attractive she was. I was also a DJ at the time, so one night, I was hanging out with my friend who owned another bar, and I actually saw her again. A mutual friend introduced us. It was cool, and we went on to talk about Stevie Wonder and other musical artists. She was so beautiful and amicable.

Our connection grew stronger and we kissed. Eventually, we started having sex (a lot at first) and then she got pregnant. Funny story is, a week before I found out that she was pregnant, I wanted to stop having sex with her. I wanted to just be friends.

Ultimately, we decided to remain friends while pursuing a family. I am his dad after all. After that, we just went from there. She said, "I know we want to be friends, but I'm committed to making this work."

When I first met her, she had straight hair. As the relationship went on, she said, "Well my hair isn't really that straight, and I'm thinking of never straightening it again because the chemicals I use to straighten my hair might affect the baby." And I was totally cool with it. It seemed like the mask came off at that point. She had the baby. Strange thing was, her boyfriend before me came the same day that the baby was born. I was trying to be mature and not think anything of it. Looking back, these were all red flags that I did not see or pay attention to.

Three weeks after she had the baby, she announced, "I'm going to Boston." I'm thinking that we're all going to Boston because the baby was just three weeks old at the time. And she was like, "No, just me." I expressed my reservations by saying, "Oh, okay. You're an adult. Whatever. I don't think it's a great idea, but whatever." After her trip, I can recall asking her how it went. She said it was horrible. She said the baby cried the whole three hours home. Of course he did; that's what babies do. I reminded her that we all should've gone together. Things got progressively worse after that.

As I look back on it, I was in denial about it. Sex stopped probably when he was around three. The odd thing is that we never argued. That was so strange to me as it was a contrast to other relationships I had. There were no arguments. I thought this was cool. In 2006, when my son was born, I realized that she might have postpartum depression and after-birth complications. She would get really snappy, and I noticed things that didn't seem indicative of her behavior. Her reactions were like Dr. Jekyll and Mr. Hyde. I mentioned that she might need to go see someone. Right after she had the baby, I said, "Hey, you should go talk to someone." It turns out that she didn't go see the doctor until it was too painful. When she went in, the doctor saw that they sewed gauze into her body. I'm like, "Dude you could have died from that. That's toxic shock syndrome right there. We need to sue them." She just brushed me off and said it wasn't a big deal.

After all of this, I was going to a therapist. I had been going since I was thirty-six years old. Because she was on this pendulum so often, she was not a happy person. We weren't having sex at all. She would lash out. The most toxic part was the silent treatment. I would agree with anything she wanted, or else anything I had criticism for I would be shut down or ignored. I didn't notice how bad it had gotten. It was to the point where I was hanging out with only her friends or her family. It was not cool. She never said that she didn't like my mother, but she made a point to never be around. It slowly dwindled off where my son's mother was never there for anything to do with my family. There were so many patterns of alienation in our relationship.

After I had done all my research on narcissism and personality disorders, I realized that there was a common thread of abuse. I didn't connect the dots before because this relationship was totally opposite to all the relationships I had ever had. They were visible. They were auditory. You could see and hear them. With this relationship, you could only feel it because arguments didn't exist.

Everyone is looking for a partnership and human connection. It's our human nature. I was looking for a true companion, someone to grow with.

The silent treatment: When you don't comply with what a person says, and they don't have the skills to communicate how they are actually feeling and work it out. You can feel the tension, but it's still nonexistent. Last week, she said, "Hey, let's create an email so we can have access to our son's homework." I thought it was a great idea and agreed. She created a long, awkward email address. She told me that she worked really hard on putting the mail together. I simply said okay because I know how she is. I came up with a more simple email because I knew that it could be difficult to remember or give out the email address over the phone. Stuff like that happens all the time. I didn't explain any of this, of course. Then she mentioned that she put in a lot of work into the calendar. I didn't tell her that she didn't put work into it, but I did say, "You could export this into the calendar of the email address that we agree on." It was an accumulation of these little tiny microaggressions. This is how they feel about themselves. It's the progression of how the other person feels.

It's like when someone gives you the cold shoulder. They don't acknowledge your presence. It's a form of passive aggression, and it makes you feel like absolute shit. You don't have anyone with checks and balances. It's despicable and horrible. It makes you ruminate and think of all the possible things you did wrong. It destroyed my self-worth and self-esteem. It felt emasculating to be ignored. To have every suggestion I made be ignored.

It makes you question yourself. If you don't have healthy individuals around you, you're going to wonder what's wrong with you. You love this person and you want them to like you. How can you get this person to like you? You do things to make them like you. After a while, you realize that it doesn't matter what you do. You become indifferent. That's what I did.

To heal, I moved out. I read a lot of books. I changed therapists. I started really educating myself on emotional abuse and manipulation and narcissism. I listened to a lot of audio books on toxic behaviors. I also got rid of a lot of people in my circle. I needed to be around people who would hear me and be there for me. I started reading books about vulnerability, guilt, shame, narcissism, and then I stumbled upon personality disorders. I spoke with a friend who was a psychologist. I began being more deliberate in my attentiveness of other people. I practiced the things I'd been learning: listening, being aware, and watching for those red flags.

Think about what your core troubles are. Latch onto the people who are willing to sit there and listen to you and your troubles. These are your safe people. Appreciate them because they are vital to your survival.

I'm not dead. I didn't take myself out. That's the important part. I don't do drugs as much, and I don't drink as much. Yes, I had depression due to the detrimental nature of my relationship. And I still have trouble speaking to women, but I see men who have gone through many of the same things I have who have drank themselves to death. I'm still alive. My greatest accomplishment is still being on this planet.

It's important to remember that abuse is not gender-specific. It's not all men are this, all women are that. It's about toxic behaviors. What I want to convey to people is that emotional health should be as important as looks. We go to the gym because we want our physique to look the best, however, where are the people focusing on feeling the best? We watch shows to learn to makeover our face, but who's making over our emotions? This is not gender specific. It affects all humans. We need to become emotionally articulate, so we can express who we are and practice vulnerability and intimacy. And that's where the real happiness and artistry of a connection lies. Working on ourselves physically is important, but the most important thing is bettering ourselves from within.

THE LESSON: MY LEGACY IS WHO I AM

I'm just here to be an example to others. Be a human being of integrity. Be a person of your word. Hey, you can fuck up and make mistakes. Everyone does. But my purpose here is to be a man of integrity and own up to my responsibilities. I want to be a person of my word. I never really looked at what my legacy is before, but the important thing is, I'm finding it out every day.

My son and I don't live together. I get four days a month with him, while his mom gets twenty-six days. I'm not knocking my ex or anything, but I do address it when I'm with him. I try to teach him confidence and self-esteem and how to be emotionally articulate. I try to give him that safe space to let him be inquisitive. He's had his own emotional trauma from being around me and his mother. I've apologized to him for that. We talk about boundaries. That's part of this behavior as well. That's what I teach my son. As I learn things, I try to share it with him. I try to keep it as real as possible. It's knowing that these things happen, and it's not our fault because your parents didn't know. I try to teach him how to navigate relationships and guide his way through this world. Toxicity can come in all sorts of shapes and sizes. It's about nurturing an emotionally healthy human being. I want to instill in him that he can be whoever he wants to be and to be a person of integrity at the end of the day.

Dissecting and Demystifying Emotional Trauma and Abuse

BY DR. ROSELYN AKER-BLACK

If we are lucky enough, we will all get the opportunity to experience love at least once in this lifetime. But if you do not know your attachment style, you may find yourself in a series of dysfunctional relationships! In all of our educational endeavors, how to love someone appropriately is never taught! Instead, our parents or caretakers are our first teachers, and how they love, nurture, and raise us is typically how many of us learn to love!

What exactly does this all mean, and why is it important for us to know our attachment styles? Once you know how you attach or emotionally bond to people, you are better able to see the red flags and recognize whether a potential relationship is safe for you!

Attachment theory suggests that bonding occurs through a set of learned behaviors, responsiveness, and care from our parents or caretakers. Four distinct attachment styles are used to describe the care that we received as infants, which in turn taught us how to respond to the world and form interpersonal relationships with others. Here's where you should take notes, as this information will help you determine your relationship personality and start you on the path to healing!

1. **SECURE** attachment is our first attachment style, and it is simply what it suggests! Children who are raised in a secure environment have responsive parents that efficiently tend to the child's needs and make the child feel safe and secure. These children become adults who are not afraid to explore the world because they have been taught there is a safety net. They are able to develop meaningful relationships and exhibit trust and empathy readily. These are the type of individuals that make great life partners.

   Cliff and Claire Huxtable are the perfect example of demonstrating what a secure and healthy relationship looks like. They created a stable home, provided guidance, and disciplined together as a couple towards their children. Although they were both professionals, they demonstrated that their children were more important than anything in the world.

2. **AVOIDANT** is our second attachment style, and it suggests that parents were neglectful, unavailable, and rejecting of their child. Whether it was due to postpartum, sickness, or the adult's inability to properly care for the child, it created an environment of mistrust in meeting the child's needs. Children raised in this environment desire the closeness of their parent, but learn they will be rejected. They cannot depend on their parents to make them feel safe and secure. As a result, they become adults that avoid closeness or emotional closeness. They can be distant, rigid, critical, and intolerant of others. They have great difficulty trusting others.

   Mr. Big from Sex in the city is a classic example of an avoidant attachment style. He loved Carrie, but their whole relationship consisted of him running away from her when they got too close. Even in heated or emotional situations, he appeared to be able to turn off his feelings and not react. Now this doesn't suggest that he did not want the relationship; he just did not have the capacity to modulate his emotions, so avoiding the relationship allowed him to avoid the anxiety of loving someone that may possibly reject him.

3. **AMBIVALENT** is our third style, and it suggests that these children were raised in an inconsistent environment with sometimes-intrusive parent communication and being overbearing with their affection. The individuals exhibit anxious, insecure, and unpredictable erratic behaviors. They tend to always blame others and never take responsibility for their part in a conflict. They desire intimacy, but they push people away with their behaviors because they fear their partner's rejection. Their behavior can often result in being displayed as clingy.

   A Thin Line Between Love and Hate is a perfect example of the ambivalent attachment style. Lynn Whitfield was masterful in showing the mindset of, "If I can't have you, no one will."

4. **DISORGANIZED** is our final attachment style. Disorganized parents ignored or were not able to meet their child's needs. These parents would exude frightening behavior and would be abusive towards their children. As a result, these individuals are chaotic, insensitive, abusive, explosive, prone to outbursts, and untrusting even though they are craving security.

   Ike and Tina Turner are a great example of this type of explosive relationship. Ike's fragile ego could not handle Tina's success, and his only way to try to diminish her greatness was through abuse. While he loved her and craved to be in a relationship with her, his emotional capacity was too disorganized to develop and maintain a trusting and loving relationship with Tina.

Right now, you must have an honest moment with yourself and assess how you emotionally attach to people. We attach to what is comfortable and familiar to us, and typically when we are in abusive adult relationships, we have experienced some level of the mistreatment before. Either you have witnessed it, been the recipient of the behavior, or you have been the perpetrator of the behavior. As a result, subconsciously this behavior may appear to be normal and generally the behavior becomes acceptable. For example, we may make an excuse when someone takes their anger out on us verbally or physically by saying they are under a lot of stress at work. As a result, making excuses for bad behavior maintains the behavior and provides permission for the maintenance of the abuse cycle.

Creating a healthy relationship means that you can not turn a blind eye to unhealthy behavior. Many victims that have escaped from an abusive relationship often state that the red flags were present once they realized what the red flags were. The truth of the matter is that we may experience different red flags based on our attachment style, but there are some red flags that are universal of the abusive cycle regardless of your attachment style. Below are a few telling signs that you should become familiar with to ensure you are safeguarding yourself against a toxic relationship.

LOVE BOMBING: Love bombing consists of when an individual falls in love with you the first day. They are professing their love publicly the first week, super attentive, charming, place you on a pedestal, profess that they have never felt this way about anyone, and...you just met seventy-two hours ago. Perpetrators have learned that we all desire to be loved, and they provide an overabundance of love and charm so quickly that you do not have an opportunity to stop and think things through logically about whether this person is a great fit for you. They provide instant security and appear to meet your needs while manipulating your emotions and your regular safeguards that you would normally have in the progression of a healthy relationship.

TIME MANIPULATION: As a part of love bombing, they want all of your time! In the beginning of a relationship, it is quite natural to want to spend time together, but when you are made to feel guilty about needing space or doing your everyday routine, your time is being manipulated. Perpetrators will do it under the guise of quality time, but it is more about controlling you and what you are doing and manipulating you to do exactly what the perpetrator wants you to do.

GASLIGHTING: Gaslighting refers to creating a situation where the person is made to feel like their reality is becoming unglued. A perpetrator will create a scenario in which the victim begins to second guess their decisions, intuition, and doubt their own perceptions. Perpetrators love to see their prey in a frenzy so that they can miraculously save them from their hysteria making the victim feel as if they can only trust them. The perpetrator must be the hero, even when they have created the chaos.

LYING: Lying becomes so effortlessly for perpetrators, and the lies are often very elaborate. Upon hearing the lie, the victim may question the validity, but the gaslighting and love bombing may keep you from fully investigating because you want to give the benefit of the doubt. Perpetrators often forget their lies, will create more lies to cover their tracks, and will opt to accuse the victim of not believing or supporting them or questioning the victim's love for them.

GLIMPSES OF ANGER: Perpetrators are savvy enough to not have a full blown anger meltdown in the beginning with their victim, however due to their difficulty with anger management, they will display their anger towards others. For example, becoming completely unhinged if someone bumps into them accidentally. Normal behavior would simply say excuse me, apologize, and move on, but not with someone that has the tendency to function in an abusive way. A situation as such would cause for "a scene" and the victim is often trying to calm them down or pull them away from an altercation. What angers them becomes unpredictable and often appears to be an overreaction.

CONDESCENDING OR "JOKING": Emotionally abusive perpetrators function in the realm of condescending their victims, and physical abusers start with being condescending towards their victims. In the beginning, they may say something about their victim in a teasing manner, or as a joke, but eventually it develops into full blown criticism. The perpetrator's insults often give them power in the relationship because the victim often will begin to believe the insults, thus affecting their self-esteem, belief about themselves, and thinking that no one else will love them.

BLAME SHIFTING: Nothing is ever the perpetrator's fault! They never take responsibility for their actions, and someone else or the victim made them behave in that manner. They struggle with the ability of seeing the consequences of their behavior, and they are often impulsive. They will not ever admit to wrongdoing, even if the evidence is present.

All of these red flags are the path to being engaged in the four stages of the abuse cycle. Once the perpetrator has the victim reeled in, they will begin to show their true colors, thus, creating the abuse cycle. The stages are as follows:

TENSION BUILDING: Perpetrators are unpredictable, so the tension can last for minutes, days, or months. A stressful environment is created, and the victim is often "walking on eggshells" to either brace for the impact or try to minimize the abuse.

ACUTE VIOLENCE: Whether physical, emotional, or psychological, the perpetrator releases the tension by an act of violence. The victim is usually blamed for the perpetrator's behavior, and both are relieved that the act is finally over.

RECONCILIATION/HONEYMOON: The abuser promises to never behave in that manner again and professes their love for the victim to either ensure that they do not leave them or call the police. The Love Bombing, showers of affection, and promises to never do harm again is so convincing to the victim and, because they hope that the situation will get better, they believe the perpetrator.

CALM: The relationship is calm and existing peacefully. The abuser may even agree to go to counseling, there are less arguments, and the victim truly begins to believe that the abuse will never occur again. The victim will let their guard down, completely forgives the perpetrator, and will stay in the relationship, thus letting the perpetrator know how to apologize in the future when it happens again.

Now that you are aware of the cycle and the red flags of an abusive relationship, you have to make a choice! If you are currently in an abusive relationship, you must choose safety! Make a plan of escape by letting those close to you know the situation you are in, document all bruises with video or pictures, protect yourself legally with restraining orders, begin to save money to reduce financial dependency, and learn skills to protect yourself. You must reconnect with your support system because your perpetrator controls you by isolating you from those that truly love you. Every city has resources to help victims. Simply just dial 211, and you will be connected to help in your city. Or reach out to the National Domestic Violence Hotline at 1-800-799-SAFE.

We all have vulnerabilities, but you must do an honest assessment of yourself to understand what makes you vulnerable prey. What is it about you that makes you an easy target to be preyed upon? Understand that this inquiry is not victim blaming, but an honest assessment about yourself to ensure that you do not present as prey anymore. You cannot heal what you avoid, and healing will require honest introspection of how you emotionally attach to others, why you attach to them in that manner, and what are you willing to do to ensure that you are functioning healthy.

Taking your power back begins with you owning your vulnerabilities, understanding how you function in your vulnerabilities, making the choice to be honest with yourself, forgiving yourself from past behaviors, and developing a plan to move differently in your relationships. Be honest about your attachment style. Once you know how you interact in relationships, you have the power to function more appropriately.

You've got this and you can do it, but you must want different life for yourself. 90 percent is becoming aware that behavior must change, and 10 percent is actually making the effort to change. Choose you, choose healthy, choose to always reassess what's driving your behavior!

EPILOGUE

About Face

I AM THE MASTER OF MY SOUL.
I AM THE AUTHOR OF MY DESTINY

-MELISSA R. HIBBÉRT-

Devastation and disappointment can be among our greatest teachers. When you are positioned to hear from yourself, the external noise turn to the white noise of peace on the inside. Learning to stand in the mirror and face myself proved to be a teachable moment. I chose to let the lessons lead me. The trauma that had so moved me transformed into worthiness. The woman who once stared at a shrinking version of herself amidst tumultuous times has since emerged from the ashes as a bonafide warrior.

The greatest sacrifice in transforming into who God has called me to be has been learning to control my emotions. I am now an empowered empath, knowing my gifts, while protecting it at the same time. I have trained myself to be emotionally intelligent but, admittedly, it was a great sacrifice. Your heart must work overtime to ensure that the outpour from you is love and love only. Emotional control also means exerting effort to suppress emotions and actions that are not in alignment with who you want to be. If you're not careful, an unhealthy partner can push you an altered emotional state for their gain. I choose today to preserve my energy for my daughter. She may never know until she is old enough to digest the contents of this book, but she was my healing space. There are times in our lives where it appears that the easiest thing to do is to lash out and to use your emotions instead of your reason. The #1 advice I received during my divorce process was, "Keep the emotions out of it." It wasn't easy, but it was necessary. Doing so comes with a price tag that no one ever truly wants to pay. The pages of this book have proven to be the outlet that I never knew that I needed. The raw depiction of emotion is what I resolved to give to every reader in hopes that this truth might have healing and restorative power. This book really could have been called *Surviving 2018*, which will go down in history as the best and the worst year of my life. Ending a short marriage while being a new Mom at the same time—there were SO many moments of my life that could've taken me out. But, they didn't.

In this very moment, and forevermore, my truth is that I ascend through transparency, healing as I reveal. Speaking the truths committed to the pages of this book took me out of my comfort zone, but it has proven to be an antidote to what will be a significant part of my legacy. It is now apparent to me, more than ever, that we are all connected; love is our destiny, and we don't find the meaning of life on our own—we find it together. Our souls yearn to attach and exchange with like energy forces. We must take heed to our internal compass that desires such connection, while paying close attention to the moments that the energy does not reproduce significantly. That means believing the "red flags" are literally a warning, setting boundaries, and never settling for less than what you deserve. When you are in alignment or "equally yoked", the souls that we connect with must foster a haven for us to be who we are, without apology, and allow us to fall into the arms of acceptance and adoration. It is then and only then do we come out of hiding of our true desires and we have access to the freedom to face the beauty that we see in the mirror as it reflects back to us, an image that proclaims, I am enough!

My heart seeks love, joy, peace, adventure, and abundance. I believe love is my birthright. I believe that being a wife and a mom is part of my legacy and that I am worthy of all good things. I am worthy of having a loving husband that covers me, protects me, and prays for me. With every passing day, I resolved to let God choose what is best for my life—the stillness and surrender is where grace saves me. I will intently listen to my life as it speaks to me and be confident that God's plan and divine timing for my life is sufficient.

I firmly believe that nothing in life is wasted. I now understand that perhaps it's not just the pain and trauma we choose to transform; it's who become after the pain and the trauma that requires the ultimate transformation. I think we owe it to ourselves to break the cycles, rewrite our own stories, take our power back, become whole again, and live worthy!

If you remember nothing else that I have resolved to share with you, please hear my humble plea: Never under any circumstances forget to Face Your Beauty. It becomes you.

The About Face Affirmation

Love and Prosperity is my birthright.

My work manifests in influence.

Abundance will find its way to me.

Joy thrives in my heart.

Clarity lingers in my soul.

I am the personification of Worthy.

Speak Your Truth and Live Worthy

WHEN YOU FACE YOUR BEAUTY, YOU RECOGNIZE THAT YOU ARE GREATER THAN ALL OF THE THINGS YOU'VE GONE THROUGH.

-MELISSA R. HIBBÉRT-

I thought long and hard about what I would say in the "afterword". As always, when I overthink, grace shows up and reminds me—all is well. So, in the words of the late, great Dr. Maya Angelou, "Develop enough courage so that you stand up for yourself and then stand up for somebody else." I never knew much of this would be my story (especially the failed marriage part of it) and I certainly wasn't sure I'd have the courage to be transparent about my personal experiences. There is beauty in being vulnerable, and I no longer feel the weight of shame. The freedom of my healing made my writing process feel cathartic. I stand in my authentic and audacious truth as a transformed woman—not a victim, but a survivor, a thriver. Every story in this book honors the resilience of people who had the courage to stand in their own truth. It is the honor for themselves. Sharing our story with you may help free old strongholds or help you to be silent no more in your own life. We were born with power in our hands to heal ourselves and the will to live our lives to the fullest. No obstacle can or will define who you are and who you can become, and the greatest lesson above all for me has been the awakening to my Worthiness. I wish someone had told me long ago that I was born worthy and that worth was not found outside of myself. The other great lesson was there is power in breaking the cycle. I learned that most people don't break the cycle, not because they don't want to, but because they don't feel worthy of it. Most of my life was spent looking to be validated by relationships and situations that were not worthy of me; I gave all of me and received very little in return. I played small often because being more than enough was offensive to other people. I wish I knew the power in what I thought was an insult being spewed by others most of my life. "She thinks she is all of that. She's full of herself." Truth is, I was showing up as worthy on the outside, but on the inside, I had undeveloped self worth and unhealed pain. A history of trauma and pain will leave you feeling the need to explain, defend, or justify who you are. And when you have the courage to walk away, it's a radical step in your ability to recognize your worth, even if you can't fully recognize it at the time. Today, I live worthy. I now set boundaries unapologetically. I continue to hold myself in high regard. I give to myself what I have spent most of my life requesting from others. I am always willing to forgive myself and to be compassionate with myself first, before I require it from anyone else. And above all else, I will never compromise my worth again, which is why I made this declaration, and it is my hope that you will also declare:

Facing your beauty denotes a deep knowing in the center of your being that you are loved and lovable. This sense of self is necessary to this life and of inestimable value and immeasurable worth.

POSTSCRIPT

Beauty Redefined

BEAUTY CAN ONLY BEGIN AT THAT MOMENT WHICH
YOU DECIDE TO LOVE YOURSELF.

-MELISSA R. HIBBÉRT

I have spent half of my life transforming faces. I want to spend the next half transforming lives. Beauty has been a blessing and has exceeded my professional desires. Every goal I have set, I have shattered. Every person I have encountered in my chair has taught me something about me, life, and our existence, so I know my purpose in beauty is bigger than makeup.

For well over a year now, I have been studying and researching the subject of "self-worth" at a time where the circumstances of my life and marriage made me feel anything but worthy. My studying essentially consisted of reading books and articles, interviewing people, and analyzing how they see and value themselves in the context of self-worth. It was mind blowing to me to essentially conclude that we live in a society of people who feel worthless and undeserving of love, joy, peace, and happiness. This simply means that I've discovered there are an abundance of people, from rich to modest, who feel essentially unworthy on some level. Many of these people tied their value to external factors, which defined their worth. But what I discovered is that self-worth is more about who you are and less about what you do.

You may find it ironic that a beauty professional who makes a living enhancing outer beauty has found her purpose in the manifestation of inner beauty. The truth is, I don't believe the two are mutually exclusive. I believe I can do both—which makes me unique! By using my own life and triumphant story, I am uniquely positioned to help a person make the connect between how they feel about themselves on the inside and how they look on the outside.

Having done the work on my own personal healing and development, I am now dedicated to helping others fall in love with themselves and to feel worthy of all good things through my "Live Worthy" coaching program, which consists of four-week online course, one-on-one coaching, intimate retreats, and ultimately, a global conference.

Speaking is a passion of mine and I believe in using my voice. I love inspiring transformation from the stage point of view and making an impact. I am excited to continue to ignite my bookings for speaking engagements with the release of this book.

On the political front, I am going to put on my pre-law/political science college degree hat I earned at Fisk University to work my way to Capitol Hill to advocate for the criminalization of emotional and psychological abuse. Victims are dying, both literally and figuratively, everyday because they are not being heard or seen. As a survivor, I know all too well feeling unworthy of protection when the system meant to defend you looks at you and says, "There are no visible scars." I want to take a moment to define emotional abuse so that if you or anyone is suffering from it, now have the awareness you need to take action to save yourself. And if you are a survivor of this abuse, you know this definition all too well. Emotional abuse is any abusive behavior that isn't physical, which may include verbal aggression, intimidation, manipulation, and humiliation. It most often unfolds as a pattern of behavior over time that aims to diminish another person's sense of identity, dignity, and self worth, and often results in anxiety, depression, suicidal thoughts or behaviors, and post-traumatic stress disorder (PTSD). Domestic abuse is an epidemic in our society, and we need more voices amplified on the epidemic of emotional and psychological abuse so that we may bring some dignity, honor, and restoration to the lives of those who suffer in silence.

Love / Support / Resources

OUR GOAL MUST NOT BE TO SIMPLY SEARCH
FOR ANSWERS, OUR GOAL MUST BE TO DISCOVER
TRUTH AND TO HEAL OURSELVES.

-MELISSA R. HIBBÉRT-

The dynamic question that we must address regarding trauma is why it happens to certain types of people. After experiencing this level of pain, it was imperative for me to seek more understanding and learn everything I can about myself, abuse, trauma, and pain. Knowledge will save you! The lightbulb moments and the Aha! moments will transform you for the better. My research and reflection has led me to many conclusions. One staggering revelation gleaned was that those of us who are considered to be empaths are often victims. Empaths are sensitive to other people's emotions and often take it on mentally and physically, often putting other feelings before their own. Being an empath is not a death sentence; it truly is a gift! We are deeply passionate, creative, compassionate, spiritual, and loyal. The major key for an empath is that we must learn to protect ourselves by setting clear limits and boundaries with toxic or draining people. We must learn that red flags are not be ignored; they are at sign to yield. We must also learn how to navigate intimate relationships without feeling suffocated—losing your breath is also a sign. For me, learning to set clear boundaries has been one of my greatest life lessons. No longer can I blame my parents by saying they didn't teach me about boundaries. Well, I am grown now, and I am responsible for my life. It's up to me to get the lesson and not repeat it. It's as if God kept having the same scenarios show up in my life (with a different face), over and over again until I got the lesson. Trust me, I did this time! Attending to the needs of others and feeling deeply for their circumstances can lead to susceptibility. Missing the warning signs and red flags of those who might prey upon us is commonplace for many who are victims of trauma. Empaths are givers by nature and, in this space, boundaries are often left to be desired. I continue to study those areas that I never understood or didn't master before. The more research that I engage in, the more I learn. It is my greatest hope that this same offering of resources can be a blessing to you or someone that you know who may find themselves amidst emotionally traumatic and toxic relationships. Most importantly, if I can save just one person from having to experience life in this way, then I know with certainty that my pain was not in vain.

My personal healing toolkit started with me first before I picked up any book. I became spiritually centered again, building back my relationship with God in an authentic way. Spiritual healing unlocked everything as I acknowledged my disobedience, asked for forgiveness, and made a commitment that I will always keep God first. Whatever your spiritual choice or faith may be, you must put that first in your life. Then, I found a good therapist who introduced me to the EMDR method. Eye Movement Desensitization and Reprocessing (EMDR) is a form of therapy that helps people heal from trauma or other distressing life experiences. She also taught me breathing techniques which are very valuable in reducing anxiety. Many trauma survivors struggle with anxiety because there is a sense of fear everywhere in the atmosphere. But with proper breathing techniques, we can be more in control of the mind. The other thing I did was fall back in love with nature. Once a week, I now commitment myself to hiking, going to the beach, walking through a garden, and literally smelling the roses. I make sure I recognize the beauty in everything—That is how I know I have healed myself because my senses are active, and they are not betraying me. Stress in the body from trauma and toxic relationships tends to throw everything off physiologically, but that doesn't have to be your story.

The listings below are the most dynamic resources that helped me to understand my experiences, heal, forgive myself and thrive.

WEBSITES:

THIS IS MY #1 RESOURCE:
Melanie Tonia Evans: Narcissism and Relationships Blog
https://blog.melanietoniaevans.com

How to Get Out of an Abusive Relationship
www.helpguide.org

Facebook Group page: Surviving Abuse: Narcissistic, Mental, Emotional

VIDEOS:

Ted Talk of Dr. Brené Brown, The Power of Vulnerability

YouTube: Bishop T.D. Jakes sermon - More Than Enough

TOP 10 BOOKS:

The Body Keeps The Score by Bessel van der Kolk M.D.

A New Earth: Awakening Your Life's Purpose by Eckhart Tolle

The Path Made Clear: Discovering Your Life's Direction and Purpose by Oprah Winfrey

Psychopath Free by Jackson MacKenzie

Boundaries: When to Say Yes, How to Say No to Take Control of Your Life by Drs. Henry Cloud and John Townsend

Red Flags of Love Fraud: 10 Signs You're Dating a Sociopath by Donna Anderson

To Be Told: Know Your Story, Shape Your Future by Dr. Dan Allender

Why Does He Do That?: Inside the Minds of Angry and Controlling Men by Lundy Bancroft

Splitting: Protecting Yourself While Divorcing Someone with Borderline or Narcissistic Personality Disorder by Bill Eddy and Randi Kreger

When Love Is A Lie: Narcissistic Partners and the Pathological Relationship Agenda by Zari L. Ballard

Contributors

ROSELYN V. AKER-BLACK, PSY.D
"DR. ROZ"
BIO

Roselyn V. Aker- Black, Psy.D (affectionately known as Dr. Roz) is a native of Rome, Georgia and currently resides in the Washington, DC metro area with her husband. Dr. Roz received a B.A. in psychology from Fisk University and completed a doctoral degree in clinical psychology at the American Schools of Professional Psychology at Argosy University in Washington, DC.

Dr. Roz is an award- winning psychologist and has over 13 years of experience in providing psychological services to children, families, and couples in the nonprofit, government, and private industry sectors. Currently, she is the Chief Operating Officer for the Goal Grinders Foundation, a nonprofit organization that provides Leadership and Entrepreneurial training with a STEM Focus for at risk middle school girls.

She also serves as a psychology professor at local universities in the DC area training nurses and the next generation of clinical and forensic psychologists. As a consultant, she serves as a Subject Matter Mental Health Expert supporting the Juvenile and Family Residential Management Unit (JFRMU) Office of Detention and Removal (DRO) of U.S. Immigration and Customs Enforcement (ICE) and as an Expert Panel member in the development of the

Health Resources and Services Administration's (HRSA), Bright Futures for Women's Health and Wellness Initiative (BFWHW); Healthy Relationships tool domain.

Dr. Roz's media experience includes psychological consults with the Anderson Cooper Talk Show (2012), the Own's Network docuseries Unfaithful (2012), Huffington Post, Fox5DC, NBC4 and a regular guest appearance on Howard University's WHUR 96.3 as a relationship expert. Dr. Roz is the Series Psychologist on TV One's limited series, "For My Woman". Dr. Aker-Black's work has also been published in International Journals.

She is a sought out key note speaker, commencement speaker, and advice columnist for her advice on practical relationship functioning, Human trafficking, Intimate Partner Violence, and Organizational Behavior and Management. She is the co-owner of Marriage Exposed, a boutique organization that is dedicated to saving marriages, as she has dedicated her life to help people function properly in relationships! Dr. Roz is also an author and co-author represented by 13th and Joan Publications.

Some of Dr. Roz's awards include the Prince George's County Social Innovation Fund Forty under Forty, The Daily Records' Very Important Professional Under Forty, Maryland's Leading Woman award , The Daily Records Top 100 Women of Maryland award, and Fisk University's Inaugural Talented Tenth award.

For bookings, Dr. Roz can be contacted at

drrozakerblack@gmail.com

https://www.facebook.com/Dr.RoselynAkerBlack

https://www.twitter.com/DrRozAkerBlack

https://www.facebook.com/DrRozakerBlack

(Public figure page)

www.IAmDrRoz.com

ABOUT
The Author

*J*amaican born Beauty Expert, Melissa R. Hibbért's love affair with all things glam started at an early age. While in her teens, Melissa began experimenting with makeup on her friends and family and decided to take cosmetology courses while completing high school in her adopted hometown of Portland, OR.

Determined to achieve a higher level of education, Melissa attended the illustrious Fisk University in Nashville, TN, where she obtained a bachelor's degree in political science and public administration. She later went on to graduate school, earning a Master's degree in Media Management. Armed with a quality education, Melissa embarked on a successful career in corporate marketing for over fourteen years, working for and with some of the leading brands in the industry such as: Nike Inc., Jordan Brand Division, BET Networks, UniWorld Group Inc., Los Angeles Times Media Group, Burger King Corporation, Ford Motors Co., and Coca-Cola to name a few. But the pull of her first love proved too strong, so she decided to shift her career path and began a journey to reinvent herself to follow her true passion: Beauty. To make her new career focus official, Melissa trained intensively under some the top celebrity makeup artists in the industry.

Through hard work and dedication to hone her craft, she is now a "go-to" beauty expert and professional makeup artist for both celebrity, corporate, and private clients alike. Her passion for flawless beauty and making every woman feel glamorous (along with her contagious enthusiasm, positive attitude, and grace) helped her to become one of the industry's most dynamic and in-demand talents. The face is her canvas, and Melissa believes every woman deserves to look as confident, powerful, and gorgeous on the outside as they feel on the inside. Melissa is squarely focused on empowering women to celebrate their uniqueness and individual beauty. Her aesthetic is to focus on "total beauty" by incorporating makeup, hair and wardrobe styling in her business strategy as a beauty professional.

Melissa was a frequent guest beauty expert on *The Real* daytime talk show on Fox for 2 years and her beauty work can be seen on OWN, BRAVO TV, Oxygen Network, Lifetime Network, WeTV, TV ONE, VH1, BET, TLC, CBS, and a variety of syndicated networks. In addition, Melissa's work has been featured in leading beauty industry publications, including several digital platforms like *Brides Magazine, Essence Magazine, Brides.com, BET.com, Essence.com, Ehow.com, YouTube*, and more. Furthermore, her work has been published on the cover and in the pages of several beauty and lifestyle magazines and is a frequent contributor to leading beauty and lifestyle blogs such as *In Her Shoes, She Runs It, Small Business Trend Setter Magazine, Mogul in the Making* and is a frequent contributor to the beauty column of *Sophisticates Black Hair Magazine*. In March 2015, the prestigious *Black Enterprise Magazine* ran two stories featuring Melissa with interviews discussing her "leap of Faith from Corporate America to Entrepreneurship" and "Empowering Women Through Beauty".

In addition to being a dynamic, professional makeup artist, Melissa is the creator and executive producer of *Behind The Glam* docu-series, and the founder of *Beauty and the Business Empowerment Conference*. Melissa embarked on a defining new venture, *The GLAM Agency*, the premier multicultural talent management firm representing leading makeup artists, hair stylists, fashion stylists, manicurists, beauty bloggers, and lifestyle experts. Her aim and focus are clear: to leave a legacy of service, empowering through beauty and inspiring the world to Live Worthy.

CONNECT WITH

Melissa R. Hibbért

WEBSITE.. www.melissahibbért.com

TWITTER... @melissahibbért

FACEBOOK... @beautybymelissahibbért

INSTAGRAM... @melissahibbért

LINKEDIN.. @melissahibbért

Face Your Beauty

Throughout her career as a leader in the beauty industry, Melissa Hibbert has transformed some of the most famous faces, in TV, film, and entertainment, while simultaneously creating successful entrepreneurial ventures. In this transparent and revealing memoir, the mogul candidly shares the most painful and traumatic experiences of her life. From overcoming childhood abandonment and surviving unhealthy interpersonal relationships to discovering her purpose to encourage a new generation to break the cycles of trauma, heal from the inside out and to live a life worthy of happiness, fulfillment, joy, and love.

Hibbért goes beyond the surface, to reveal the transformative lessons that changed her life and introduces you to five courageous and audacious survivors whose personal and traumatic stories will leave you breathless. The compilation of stories begs the question, How can we face ourselves when love turns dark and emotional abuse leaves remnants of unworthiness, and powerlessness?

As the book unfolds, answers are revealed, and the presence of transcendence guides the reader to thrive. Hibbért believes that we deep within each of us, in the very core of our being lies our truth, our power, our courage, and our worthiness. It is in this space that you have the power to Face Your Beauty.